Follo

Happy Birthday
dearest Kathleen!

With Love,
Ping Hui
7/7/96

By the same author

La testa fra le nuvole
Per voce sola
Cuore di ciccia

Susanna Tamaro

Follow Your Heart

Translated from the Italian by Avril Bardoni

Secker & Warburg LONDON

First published in Italy in 1994 as
Va' dove ti porta il cuore by Baldini & Castoldi

This translation first published in Great Britain in 1995
by Martin Secker & Warburg Limited,
an imprint of Reed Consumer Books Limited,
Michelin House, 81 Fulham Road, London SW3 6RB
and Auckland, Melbourne, Singapore and Toronto

Copyright © 1994 by Baldini & Castoldi, Milano
Translation copyright © 1995 by Avril Bardoni

Susanna Tamaro and Avril Bardoni have asserted their moral
rights

A CIP catalogue record for this book
is available from the British Library
ISBN 0 436 20323 5

Typeset by Deltatype Ltd, Ellesmere Port, Wirral

This edition first printed in Australia 1995
by Australian Print Group
Reprinted 1995

O Shiva, what is your reality?
What is this universe so full of marvels?
What makes the seed?
What is the hub of the wheel of the universe?
What is this life beyond the form that pervades all forms?
How can we enter fully into it, above space and time, names
and appearances?
Banish my doubts!

From a sacred text of Kashmiri Shiva-worship

Opicina, 16 November 1992

You have been away for two months, and for two months I have heard nothing from you apart from a postcard telling me that you were still alive. This morning I stood in the garden for a long time looking at your rose. Although we are well into autumn, it still stands out – crimson, proud and solitary – from all the other plants which are now faded and dead. Do you remember the day we planted it? You were ten years old and had just finished reading *The Little Prince*, a present from me for passing your exams. You were enchanted by the story. Your favourite characters were the rose and the wolf; but you did not like the baobab tree, the snake, the airman or the little, empty, pretentious men floating around on their minuscule planets. So one morning over breakfast, you said, 'I want a rose.' And when I argued that we already had a great many roses, you replied, 'But I want one that is all mine, I want to look after it and make it grow tall.' Naturally, you wanted a wolf as well as a rose, and with childish cunning you had expressed the more easily gratified wish before the almost impossible one. Having agreed to the rose, how could I deny you a wolf? After discussing the matter at length, we arrived at the compromise of a dog.

The day before we went to collect it you didn't sleep a wink. Every thirty minutes you were knocking on my door saying you couldn't sleep. In the morning you had breakfasted, washed and dressed before seven o'clock, and were sitting in an armchair with your overcoat on, waiting for me. By half past eight we were at the kennels, which were still closed. Peering through the gratings, you asked me, 'How shall I know which is mine?' You sounded so anxious. I reassured you, telling you not to worry and to remember how the Little Prince tamed the wolf.

We returned to the kennels on three successive days. There were more than two hundred dogs and you wanted to see them all. You stopped in front of every cage and stood still and indifferent while the dogs threw themselves at the wire mesh, barking, leaping up and down and trying to tear the netting to shreds with their paws. The woman in charge of the kennels was with us. Thinking you were a normal little girl, she tried to help you to make a decision by showing you the dogs that looked the nicest. 'How about that cocker spaniel?' she said, 'or this collie?' Your only reply was to give a kind of grunt and walk on paying her no attention.

We encountered Buck on the third day of our *via crucis*. He was in one of the pens at the back where they kept convalescent animals. When we got to the pen, instead of bounding to meet us with all the others, he remained sitting where he was, without even lifting his head. 'That one,' you said, pointing to him, 'that's the dog I want.' Do you remember the amazed look on the woman's face? She couldn't understand why you wanted such an unprepossessing brute. And can you blame her? Buck was a small dog, but his small dimensions encompassed nearly every breed of dog known to man. He had the head of a German shepherd, the soft droopy ears of a gun-dog, the slender, pointed paws of a dachshund, the plumy tail of a Welsh collie and the black and red coat of a dobermann. When we went to the office to sign the documents, the girl told us his history. He had been thrown from a moving car in early summer, hurting himself so badly that one of his back legs was permanently maimed.

Buck is beside me as I write, sighing every now and then and touching my leg with the tip of his nose. His face and ears are now almost white, and the film old dogs develop over their eyes has been affecting his for quite a while. I find the sight of him very moving. It is like having a part of you near me, the part I love most, the part that, so many years ago, made you choose the saddest and ugliest dog of all the two hundred inmates at the dogs' home.

As I have wandered aimlessly through the empty house these last few months, the misunderstandings and bad temper that marred our years together have vanished. The memories surrounding me now are of you as a child – a vulnerable, bewildered little creature. It is to this child that I am writing, not to the defensive, arrogant person of later years. The idea was suggested to me by the rose. This morning, as I walked past, it said: 'Get out your writing paper and write her a letter.' I haven't forgotten that one of the pacts we made before you left was not to write and this I shall respect, albeit reluctantly. These pages will never wing their way to you in America. If I am no longer alive when you return, they will be waiting for you. Why should I say such a thing? Because less than a month ago, for the first time in my life, I was taken seriously ill. So now I know that this is another possibility I must take into account, that in another six or seven months I may not be here to open the door for you, to embrace you. Some time ago one of my friends was saying that when illness strikes someone who has never known what it means to be ill, it does so in a very sudden and violent way. This is exactly what happened to me. One morning, while I was watering the rose, it was as if someone had switched off the light. If Mr Razman's wife had not seen me through the fence between our gardens, you would almost certainly have been an orphan by now. Orphan? Is that the right word for someone who loses a grandmother? I'm not sure; maybe grandparents are considered of such secondary importance that their loss requires no special term. Grandparents leave neither orphans nor widows. In the way of things we abandon them by the roadside as we might, from mere absentmindedness, leave an umbrella behind.

When I regained consciousness in hospital I could remember nothing at all. Before I opened my eyes I felt as if I had grown two sets of long, thin whiskers like those of a cat, but as soon as I opened them I realized that these were in fact two little plastic tubes running from my nose and across my lips. Around me was nothing but strange machines. After a few days I was moved into an ordinary ward where there were two other patients. One afternoon while I was there Mr Razman and his wife came to visit me. 'You owe your life to your dog,' they told me, 'he barked like a maniac.'

One day after I was allowed to get up, a young doctor I had seen several times on his rounds came into my room. He pulled up a chair and sat down beside my bed. 'As you have no relatives to look after you and make decisions for you,' he said, 'I must dispense with third parties and speak frankly to you.' While he spoke, I was watching rather than listening to him. He had thin lips and, as you know, I have never liked people with thin lips. According to him, my condition was so serious that I could not return home. He mentioned the names of two or three old people's homes with nursing facilities where I could go to live. He must have gathered something from the expression on my face, because he added quickly, 'Don't imagine that these are like the old type of hospice. Everything is different now, with sunny rooms and big gardens to walk in.' 'Doctor,' I said, 'do you know anything about the Eskimos?' 'Indeed I do,' he replied, getting up. 'Well then, I intend to die as they do.' He didn't seem to understand what I meant, so I added, 'I would rather fall flat on my face among the courgettes in my kitchen garden than live for an extra year bedridden in a whitewashed room.' He was on his way out, but before he disappeared he turned around with a malicious smile. 'Lots of people say that,' he said, 'but at the last moment they come running back, shaking like aspens and begging to be looked after.'

Three days later I signed a ludicrous form declaring that if I died the responsibility would be mine and mine alone. This I gave to a nurse with a small head and enormous gold earrings and then, having bundled my few possessions into a plastic carrier bag, I headed for the taxi rank.

As soon as Buck saw me at the garden gate he started to run round in circles like a mad thing; then, to demonstrate his joy unequivocally, he demolished a couple of flowerbeds while barking non-stop. For once I hadn't the heart to scold him. When he came up to me with his nose all covered with mud, I said, 'So, old friend, we're back together, aren't we?' And I scratched him behind the ears.

I did little or nothing in the days that followed. The responses down my left side are weaker since the attack. My left hand, in particular, moves very slowly. The thought of giving in to this makes me so cross that I do all I can to use that hand more than the other. I tie a red bow to my wrist so that every time I reach out for something I remember to use my left hand rather than my right. As long as our bodies function properly we don't realize what terrible enemies they can be, but if we drop our guard for a second, we're lost.

All the same, seeing that my self-sufficiency is not what it was, I have given Walter's wife a set of keys. She pops in every day to see me and gets everything I need.

As I wander around the house and garden, the thought of you has become insistent to the point of obsession. Many a time I have gone to the telephone and picked it up intending to send you a telegram. But each time, as soon as I got through to the exchange, I decided against it. In the evening, sitting in my armchair – emptiness in front of me and silence around me – I have been asking myself what I should do for the best. Best for you, naturally, not for me.

For me it would of course be much nicer to have you near me when I go. I am sure that if I had told you about my illness, you would have cut short your stay in America and rushed to me. But then what? What if I should live another three or four years, perhaps confined to a wheelchair, perhaps mentally impaired, while you cared for me dutifully? You would do so with dedication, but in time that dedication would transform itself into anger and bitterness. The bitterness would come as the years rolled by and your youth was wasted. My love would have had a boomerang effect, forcing your life into a blind alley. This was the argument used by the voice inside me that didn't want to phone you. But no sooner had I decided it was right than another voice was arguing the contrary. What would happen, I wondered, if you were to open the door and find, instead of Buck and me rushing to make a fuss of you, an empty, long-uninhabited house? Is there anything worse than a return thwarted of fulfilment? If, over there, you received a telegram informing you of my death, might you not construe it as a kind of betrayal? An act of malice? Given your lack of civility towards me during the last months, was I punishing you by going without a word? This would not have been a boomerang but an abyss, and I doubt if anyone could survive such an experience. Things you wanted to say would remain bottled up inside you for ever; the granny you loved would be buried in her grave and you could never look her in the eyes again, embrace her, say the things you hadn't said before.

   Days passed without my coming to any kind of decision. Then, this morning, the rose inspired me. Write her a letter, it said, a little record of your days that will keep her company when you are gone. So here I am in the kitchen with one of your old exercise books in front of me, chewing my pen like a schoolgirl fretting over her homework. A testament? Not precisely, but something you can keep through the years, something you can read whenever you need to feel me near you. Don't worry, I don't intend to pontificate or to upset you; only to chat with the intimacy which once bound us and which we have lost over the last few years. Because I have lived for so long and have left so many people behind me, I have come to the realization that it is not the absence of the dead that weighs on us but the words left unspoken between them and us.

You see, I was already getting on when I had to take on the role of mother to you, of an age when people expect to be no more than grandparents. There were many advantages in this. You benefited, because a 'granny-mother' is more attentive, more patient, than a 'mother-mother', and I benefited because instead of lapsing into senility with card parties and afternoons at the women's club like the rest of my age group, I was dragged back into the mainstream of life. But there came a time when something snapped. It wasn't my fault, it wasn't your fault, but nature taking its course.

Childhood and old age are very similar. In both cases, for different reasons, there is an element of defencelessness; we are either not yet, or we have ceased to be, part of the active world, and our responses can be spontaneous, open. During adolescence an invisible shell begins to harden around our bodies, and gets thicker and thicker throughout our adult life. It grows rather like the way a pearl grows: the bigger and deeper the wound, the stronger the crust becomes. However, like a dress we wear too often, with the passage of time it begins to get thin in some places until, quite unexpectedly, as the result of a sudden movement, it splits. At first, confident in the protection of your shell, you notice nothing; then something quite banal happens and, without knowing why, you find yourself crying like a baby.

This is precisely what I meant when I said that a rift had opened naturally between us. While your shell was beginning to develop, mine had already disintegrated. You could not bear my tears and I could not bear your new hardness. Although I was prepared for the fact that your character would change with adolescence, once the change had occurred I found it difficult to bear. I found myself face to face with a different person, someone I did not know how to deal with. At night, when I had gone to bed and was collecting my thoughts as one does, I felt positive about what was happening to you. I told myself that no one who goes through adolescence unscathed can develop into a real adult. But next morning, when you slammed the first door in my face, how depressing I found it, how near I was to tears! Try as I might, I could not summon up sufficient energy to stand up to you. If you live to be eighty, you will understand that people of that age feel like the leaves of a tree at the end of September. With the shortening of the days, little by little the tree is drawing its nutritious substances into itself; the trunk reabsorbs its nitrogen, chlorophyll and protein, and as they go so does the greenness, the elasticity. The leaf hangs on, but knows that it cannot do so for very long. One after another the other leaves drop; you see them fall and live in fear of the wind rising. In my case the wind was you, the confrontational vitality of your adolescence. You never realized this, did you, my darling? We were both clinging to the same tree, but in such different seasons.

I remember the day you left. What a state we were in! You wouldn't let me come with you to the airport, and every time I reminded you to pack something or other you told me, 'I'm going to America, not the desert!' As you walked through the door, I shouted in my odiously shrill voice, 'Look after yourself,' and you, without even turning round, left me with the words, 'Look after Buck and the rose.'

At the time, I must confess, your words left me with a deep sense of frustration. Sentimental old woman that I am, I had expected something more banal: a kiss or a word or two of affection. Only later that night, when I had given up trying to sleep and was wandering round the empty house in my dressing gown, did I understand that looking after Buck and the rose meant looking after the part of you that still lives with me – the happy part. I also realized that what had made you speak so sharply was not insensitivity but the strain of holding back your tears. This is the shell I mentioned. Yours is so tight around you that you can hardly breathe. Do you remember what I told you several times during those last months? The tears we do not shed settle in and around the heart, and as time goes by they form a crust which paralyses it, like lime-scale in a washing machine.

I know, my homely similes based on the lore of the kitchen will bore rather than amuse you. You must put up with them; everyone culls inspiration from whatever is most familiar.

Now I must stop. Buck is sighing and looking at me imploringly. He too is an example of the rhythms of nature. Whatever the season, he knows so precisely when it's time for a meal that you could set your watch by it.

18 November

Last night it rained very heavily, so heavily that the noise of the rain against the shutters woke me several times. When I opened my eyes this morning I saw the weather was still bad so I stayed snuggled up in bed for quite a time. How things change with the passing years! At your age I was like a dormouse; if no one woke me I was capable of sleeping until lunchtime. But now I invariably wake before dawn, and this makes the days so long, so interminably long. There's something cruel about this, don't you think? Apart from anything else, the morning hours are the worst of the day because there are no distractions and you are driven in upon yourself knowing that your every thought can only be of the past. An old person's thoughts have no future, they are for the most part sad, or if not sad at least melancholy.

I have often wondered about this strange aspect of nature. The other day I saw a documentary that made me think. They were talking about the dreams of animals. From the birds upwards through the natural hierarchy, all animals apparently dream a lot. Tom-tits and pigeons, rabbits and squirrels, dogs and the cows lying in the fields ... they all dream but not all in the same way. Animals naturally preyed upon by other animals have very short dreams, apparitions rather than dreams as such. Predators, on the other hand, have long and complicated dreams. 'For animals,' the narrator explained, 'dreams are a way of organizing strategies for survival. Hunters are always having to work out new methods of catching their food, while the hunted – whose food is normally right in front of them in the shape of grass – have only to think about the swiftest means of escape.' So while a sleeping antelope sees the open plain stretching in front of it, a sleeping lion sees, in a series of scenes repeated with variations, all the things it will have to do before it can eat the antelope. So, I was thinking, we must be carnivores when we are young and herbivores when we are old. Because old people, apart from not sleeping very much, do not dream, or maybe, if they do, they forget their dreams. Children and young people, on the other hand, dream much more, and their dreams are vivid enough to determine the mood of the whole day.

Do you recall how often you woke up crying during those last few months? You sat with your coffee on the table in front of you and tears rolling silently down your cheeks. 'Why are you crying?' I asked you, and you – sometimes bleakly, sometimes angrily – answered, 'I don't know.' At your age so much is going on in your mind that has to be sorted out. You have projects, and projects mean uncertainty. The unconscious has no order or clear logic; it mixes the crumbs of the day, swollen or distorted as they may be, with the highest hopes and aspirations, and among the highest aspirations it interposes the needs of the body. So if someone is hungry, they dream of sitting at a table without being able to eat, if they are cold they may find themselves at the North Pole without an overcoat, if they have been insulted they become bloodthirsty warriors. What are you dreaming about over there among the cactus and the cowboys? How I should love to know. I wonder, do I sometimes make an appearance, perhaps in the skins of a Red Indian squaw? Does Buck appear, disguised as a coyote? Do you get homesick? Do you think of us?

Yesterday evening, incidentally, while I was reading in my armchair, I heard a rhythmical sound in the room and raising my eyes from the book saw Buck thumping his tail on the floor as he slept. From the blissful expression on his face, I am certain that he saw you there in front of him. Perhaps you had just returned and he was making a fuss of you, or maybe he was reliving a particularly nice walk you'd had together. Dogs are amazingly susceptible to human emotion; living with us from the dawn of history, they have grown to be like us. That is why so many people dislike them intensely: they see too much of themselves reflected in the slavishly affectionate eyes, things they would prefer not to know. Buck has often dreamt about you lately. I would like to but cannot, or maybe I do but can't remember.

When I was a little girl, one of my father's sisters lived with us for a time after the death of her husband. She was an ardent spiritualist, and whenever my parents were out of the way she would take me into the darkest, most secret corners of the house and tell me about the extraordinary powers of the mind. 'If you want to make contact with someone far away,' she would say, 'you must clasp their photograph in your hand, make the shape of a cross by taking three paces and then say, "Here I am." ' According to her, I could communicate telepathically with anybody I wanted to.

This afternoon, before I started to write, I did just that. It was about five o'clock. It would have been morning where you are. Did you see me? Or hear me? I saw you in one of those bars full of lights and tiles where they serve rolls stuffed with cooked meat; I picked you out at once from the multicoloured crowd because you were wearing the last jersey I knitted for you, the one with the red and blue stags on it. The image, however, was so fleeting and so similar to those in a film on television that I had no time to see the expression in your eyes. Are you happy? That's what I care about more than anything else.

Do you remember how long we argued about the rights and wrongs of my financing your lengthy studies abroad? You maintained that it was absolutely essential for you, that if your mind were to grow and broaden you had to get away from the stifling surroundings in which you had been brought up. You had just left school and had no idea of what you were going to do in the adult world. As a child you had so many different passions. You wanted to be a vet, an explorer, a children's doctor working among the poor. All these passions faded without trace. The initial openness you had shown towards your fellow beings was diminishing; everything that had once tended towards philanthropy and the desire to be one of the community was, in a very short time, transmuted into cynicism, solitariness, an obsession with your own unhappy destiny. If we happened to see anything particularly cruel on television, you would scoff at my compassion, saying, 'At your age, why should anything surprise you? Don't you know yet that natural selection is the governing principle of the world?'

The first time you made this sort of remark I was dumbfounded; it seemed to me that there was a monster sitting beside me. Looking at you out of the corner of my eye, I asked myself where you had sprung from and if this was what I had taught you by my own example. I never answered you on these occasions, however, having realized that the time for debate was past and that whatever I said would only result in a confrontation. On the one hand I was afraid of my frailty, of the useless expenditure of energy; on the other I sensed that an open confrontation was exactly what you were hoping for, that the first would have been followed by others, more frequent and ever more violent. Behind your words I perceived a seething energy, an arrogant energy ready to explode, held back only with difficulty. My smoothing the rough edges and feigning indifference to the attacks forced you to find other outlets for this energy.

That was when you threatened to go away, to disappear out of my life and never see me or write to me again. Perhaps you were hoping for the desperation, the humble supplications of an old woman. When I told you that it was an excellent idea for you to go away, you began to waver; you were like a snake which, having raised its head with its mouth open ready to strike, sees nothing to attack. So you began to negotiate, to make one suggestion after another, all of them vague until the day when you announced with a new-found confidence over coffee: 'I'm going to America.'

I greeted this decision, as I had done the others, with friendly consideration. The last thing I wanted was to feel that my approval was forcing you into a hasty decision you were not 100 per cent sure about. In the weeks that followed you continued to talk about the idea of going to America. 'If I can go there for one year,' you said repeatedly and almost obsessively, 'at least I shall learn another language and won't be wasting time.' You became extremely irritated when I pointed out that wasting time wasn't such a bad thing, but your irritation knew no bounds when I said that life is not a race but an archery contest. Saving time counts for nothing; what matters is to hit the bull's-eye. There were two cups on the table; you sent them crashing to the floor with a sweep of your arm before bursting into tears. 'You're stupid,' you said, burying your face in your hands. 'You're stupid. Can't you see that's just what I want?' For weeks we had been like two soldiers who had buried a land-mine in a field and were being careful not to tread on it. We knew where it was and what it was, and were walking apart from each other pretending that what we were afraid of was something quite different. When it finally exploded and you were sobbing as you told me I knew nothing and never would know anything, it was all I could do to stop you seeing how upset I was.

I have never told you about your mother, the circumstances surrounding your conception and her death, and my silence has led you to believe that these things were of no account to me. But your mother was my daughter. You may have overlooked this fact, or perhaps, instead of talking about it, you keep it bottled up inside you, which is the only explanation I can think of for the way you sometimes look at me and for the hate I hear in your voice. Apart from the gap in your life, you have no memories of her; you were only a tiny child when she died. But I have thirty-three years of memories, thirty-three years plus the nine months I carried her in my womb.

How could you think that I felt nothing about all this?

I never tackled the subject before simply because of shyness and an inflated ego. Shyness because it was inevitable that in speaking of her I should have to speak of myself and of my guilt, real or imputed; egoism because I hoped my love was so great that you would never miss hers, never feel the need to ask me one day, 'Who was my mother, and why did she die?'

While you were a child, we were happy together. You were a happy child, but your happiness was never superficial or synthetic. It was a happiness always in danger of falling prey to contemplation, and you could pass from laughter to silence with astonishing ease. 'What's the matter? What are you thinking about?' I used to ask when this happened, and you would reply, as lightly as if we were discussing what to have for tea, 'I'm wondering if the sky ends somewhere or goes on for ever.' I was proud of you for this, your sensitivity was very like my own; I was conscious not of the difference in our ages or any distance between us but only of an affectionate partnership. I deluded myself, or wanted to delude myself, that it would always be like that. But unfortunately we are not suspended in soap bubbles, floating happily through the air. There is a before and an after in our lives, and between this before and after our fate is trapped and held as if in a net.

They say that the sins of the fathers are visited upon the children. It is true, it is absolutely true: the sins of the fathers do fall upon the children, those of the grandparents fall upon the grandchildren, those of the great-grandparents upon the great-grandchildren. Some truths are liberating, others terrifying. This falls into the latter category. Where does the chain of guilt begin? With Cain? Can things possibly go back so far? Is there something behind it all? I once read in a book of Indian philosophy that fate possesses all the power, and we only imagine that will can make any difference. When I read this my soul was filled with peace. But the very next day I read, a few pages on, that fate is nothing but the result of our past actions, that it is we who forge our destiny with our own hands. So I was back to square one. Where, I wondered, is the key to all this? Which thread will unravel the skein? And is it a thread or an iron chain? Can we cut it, or break it, or are we bound by it for ever?

And talking about breaking, I must break off now. My brain is not what it was; the ideas are still there, no doubt about that, and my views are unchanged, but not my ability to sustain long effort. I'm weary now, my head is spinning as I remember it doing when, as a girl, I tried to read a book about philosophy. Being, not-being, immanence . . . a few pages were enough to make my head feel as dizzy as if I were riding in a coach along mountain roads. I must leave you for now, and let that dear odious box in the sitting-room lull me into imbecility.

20 November

Here we are again, on day three of our encounter. Or rather, day four although we have only met on three days. Yesterday I was so tired that I could neither read nor write a word. I was restless, and not knowing what to do with myself I spent the whole day wandering about the house and garden. The air was mild, and in the warmest part of the day I sat on the bench by the forsythia. All around me, lawn and flowerbeds were in an absolute mess. Looking at it, I remembered our quarrel over sweeping up dead leaves. When was that? Last year? Two years ago? I'd had bronchitis and couldn't seem to shake it off, but the lawn was covered with fallen leaves eddying in the wind. Looking out of the window at the dark sky and the scene of desolation, I had been gripped by a feeling of tremendous sadness. I came to your room and found you lying on your bed with headphones clamped to your ears. I asked if you would please rake up the leaves. I had to repeat myself several times, each time louder than the last, before you heard me. You shrugged your shoulders and said, 'Why on earth? In the natural world no one sweeps up the leaves. They lie on the ground until they rot and that's what they're supposed to do.' At the time, the natural world was your great ally, its immutable laws providing an excuse for everything. Instead of explaining that a garden is a part of the natural world that has been domesticated, a nature-dog that grows more and more like its master with the years and needs continual attention just like a dog, I retreated to the sitting-room without saying another word. When, shortly afterwards, you passed close to me on your way to the kitchen to raid the fridge, you saw that I was crying but chose to ignore it. Not until you came out of your room again at supper time and asked, 'What's for supper?' did you notice that I was still in the same place, still crying. So you went to the kitchen and started busying yourself around the stove. 'Which would you prefer,' you shouted from there, 'a chocolate pudding or an omelette?' You had realized that I was genuinely upset and were trying to be sweet, to do something to please me. As soon as I opened the shutters the next morning I saw you out on the lawn in the pouring rain, wearing the yellow oilskin and raking up the leaves. When you came indoors at around nine o'clock, I said nothing, knowing there was nothing you detested more than the side of your nature that inspired goodness and gentleness.

Looking sadly at the flowerbeds this morning, I was thinking that it really is time I got someone in to deal with the state of neglect into which the garden has slipped since my illness. I've been thinking about it ever since I came out of hospital, but have still not made up my mind. Over the years I have become very jealous where the garden is concerned, and not for anything in the world would I allow anyone else to water the dahlias or pluck a dead leaf from a branch. This is strange, because I used to find gardening such a bore when I was young, and thought that having a garden was more of a chore than a privilege. I only had to relax my vigilance for a day or two and all the order achieved with so much hard work started lapsing into disorder once again. And nothing got on my nerves so much as disorder. I had no focal point within myself, so a similar state of affairs in the external world was unbearable. I should have remembered that when I asked you to rake up the leaves!

Some things cannot be understood until we reach a certain age. Among these is the relationship with one's home and everything within and around it. When you get to sixty or seventy, you suddenly realize that the house and garden are no longer a house and a garden where you live for the sake of convenience or because they are pretty, but they are your house and your garden, they are part of you in the same way that its shell is part of the creature inside it. You have built the shell with your own secretions, your history is inscribed within its spirals; the house-shell envelops you, it is above you and around you and perhaps not even your death will free it of your presence, of the joys and griefs you experienced within it.

Yesterday evening I didn't want to read, so I watched television. Though to tell the truth I was listening to it rather than watching it, because I fell into a kind of doze less than half an hour into the programme. I heard scraps of speech, rather like you do when you half nod off on the train and catch disjointed bits of your fellow travellers' conversations but not enough to make sense of them. They were showing a debate between journalists about late twentieth-century sects. There were interviews with various gurus, genuine and fake, and in the torrent of words 'karma' cropped up several times. It immediately conjured up the face of my philosophy teacher at school.

He was a young man and, for his time, daringly unconventional in his views. While expounding Schopenhauer, he had spoken a bit about oriental philosophies and in so doing had introduced us to the concept of karma. At the time I didn't pay much attention to it; the word and its definition went in one ear and out the other. For many years I had a vague idea in the back of my mind that it was some kind of *lex talionis*, of the eye for an eye and tooth for a tooth variety, as you do unto others so will it be done unto you. Karma – and everything connected with it – only resurfaced in my mind the day your nursery school teacher phoned to tell me about your odd behaviour. You had set the entire school in an uproar. Right out of the blue, in a lesson devoted to story-telling, you had begun to talk about your previous life. To begin with, the teachers thought it no more than some infantile aberration. They tried to belittle your story, to trap you into contradictions. But you refused to be trapped, and even said some words in a completely unknown language. When the same thing happened for the third time, the headmistress sent for me. For your own good and for your future protection, she advised me to send you to a psychiatrist. 'After all she's been through,' she said, 'it's quite natural that she should behave in such a way, that she should escape into a fantasy world.' Of course I never took you to a psychiatrist. You were, it seemed to me, a happy child, and I was more inclined to believe that your flights of fantasy had their origin not in any hardship that you were suffering but in something quite different. After the incident I never tried to coerce you into talking about it, and you for your part never felt the need to do so. You may even have forgotten the day you spoke about it to your terrified teachers.

I have the feeling that over the past few years it has become fashionable to speak about such things. Time was when they were only discussed among the chosen few, but now they are on everyone's lips. Some time ago I read an article that said that in America there are even self-awareness groups focusing on reincarnation. People meet to discuss their past lives. A housewife might say, 'In the nineteenth century I was a prostitute in New Orleans; that's why I can't be faithful to my husband,' while the racist petrol-pump attendant explains his hatred for black people by saying that he was devoured by the Bantu during an expedition in the sixteenth century. What foolishness, and how sad! Having lost touch with the roots of their own culture, people try to make up past lives to compensate for the greyness and insecurity of the present. If the cycle of life has a meaning, I am sure it is something quite different from this.

When the nursery school incident occurred, I got hold of some books so that by knowing more I could understand you better. And in one of those articles I read that children who have a clear memory of a past life are those who met with a premature and violent end. Certain obsessive fears for which I could see no explanation in your childhood experience – such as gas coming out of the pipes and your being afraid of its exploding from one moment to the next – made me wonder about this kind of explanation. When you were tired or anxious or asleep and therefore with your guard down, you were sometimes seized by a quite irrational terror. It wasn't fear of the bogyman or witches or werewolves, but a sudden fear that the whole physical universe might explode. On the first few occasions when this happened and you appeared, terrified, in my room at the dead of night, I got up and comforted you and then took you back to bed. Lying there holding my hand, you asked me to tell you a story with a happy ending. Afraid I might say something that disturbed you, you would offer a detailed synopsis and I would follow your instructions obediently to the letter. I would repeat the story two or even three times, then, when I got up to go, convinced that you had calmed down, your sleepy little voice would stop me in the doorway, saying, 'Is that how it goes? Does it really always end like that?' So I would return and as I kissed your forehead I would say, 'There's no other way it can end, my darling, I promise you.'

Other nights, however, although I didn't want to let you sleep with me (children should never sleep with old people) I hadn't the heart to send you back to your own bed. As soon as I knew you were standing there by the bedside table, I didn't turn round but I reassured you: 'Everything's under control, nothing's going to explode, you can go back to your own room.' Then I pretended to fall fast asleep. For a little while I could tell from the sound of your soft breathing that you were standing there motionless, but then the side of the bed would give a little creak as you climbed in as softly as possible and snuggled up close to me before falling into an exhausted sleep like a little mouse that has reached his warm burrow after a bad fright. Come the dawn, not to spoil the game, I carried you, all warm and sound asleep, to your own room. You seldom remembered anything when you woke up, but were nearly always convinced that you had spent the whole night in your bed.

When you were attacked by these feelings of panic during the day, I used to speak to you very gently. 'See how solid the house is,' I said, 'and how thick the walls are. How could they possibly explode?' But all my attempts to reassure you were in vain. You gazed wide-eyed in front of you, repeating, 'Anything can explode.' I never ceased wondering about this terror of yours. What was this explosion? Could it be the memory of your mother, of her sudden and tragic death? Or did it have something to do with that life you described in such a strangely matter-of-fact way to your teachers at school? Who can tell? In spite of everything they say, I believe that there is still more darkness than light in the human mind. The book I bought at the time also said that children who remember past lives are much more numerous in India and the Orient, those countries where the concept is traditionally accepted. This I can easily believe. Just think what would have happened had I gone to my mother one day and started speaking without warning in a strange language; or supposing I had said to her, 'I don't like you; I was much better off with the mother I had in my previous life.' You can be sure that she would have had me shut up in a lunatic asylum before the day was out.

Is there any way of freeing ourselves from the fate dictated by childhood environment or heredity? Who knows? Perhaps in the claustrophobic succession of the generations someone, at some point, will espy a step fractionally higher than the others and try resolutely to climb it. To break out of the circle, to bring fresh air into the room – this, I believe, is the minuscule secret of the cycle of life. Minuscule but exhausting, and terrifying because of its uncertainty.

My mother married when she was sixteen, and had me when she was seventeen. Not once during my childhood or indeed throughout my whole life, did I ever see her show one sign of affection. Hers was not a love-match. No one had forced her into it, she had forced herself, mainly because, although wealthy, she was a Jewess and a converted one moreover, and she coveted a title. My father, older than she, a baron and a music-lover, was enchanted with her talent as a singer. Having procreated the heir required to perpetuate the good name of the family, they spent the rest of their lives despising and being spiteful to each other. My mother died a bitter, unsatisfied woman, never having had the remotest suspicion that any part of the fault for this could have been laid at her door. It was the world that had treated her cruelly by not offering her a better chance. I was very different from her, and by the time I was seven and no longer a helpless infant, I had already begun to hate her.

I suffered greatly because of her. She was always

agitated, and invariably about external things. Her own presumed 'perfection' made me feel that I was bad, and the result of my badness was isolation. To begin with I tried to be like her, but my attempts were clumsy and always ended in disaster. The more I tried, the more uneasy I felt. Failure leads to loss of self-esteem, and from there to anger is but a short step. Once I had realized that my mother's love was bound up with externals only, with what she wanted me to be rather than what I was, I began, in the privacy of my room and the secrecy of my heart, to loathe her.

To escape from this emotion I took refuge in a world of my own. In bed at night, with a cloth over the lamp, I read adventure books into the small hours. I loved day-dreaming. There was a period when I dreamt I was a pirate on the China Sea, but a very special kind of pirate because the money I stole was not for myself but all for the poor. Pirates and bandits eventually gave way to dreams of philanthropy; I thought I might become a doctor and go to Africa to look after little black children. When I was fourteen, I read Schliemann and realized that I would never ever be able to cure people because my great passion was for archaeology. Out of the infinite number of activities I imagined myself undertaking, this was perhaps the only one that would have been truly right for me.

And in fact, to achieve this ambition, I fought my one and only battle with my father. It was over whether I should or should not go to grammar school and receive a classical education. He was very much against it, saying that there was no point in it and that if I really wanted to study, languages would be more useful. In the end, however, I prevailed, and when I left middle-school I was confident of victory. I was mistaken. When, after finishing at grammar school, I told him that I intended to go to the University of Rome, his reply was categorical: 'I won't even discuss it.' And, as was the custom in those days, I obeyed without a murmur. One should never think that winning a battle is the same as winning a war. That is a childish error. Thinking about it now, I feel that had I insisted, had I dug my heels in, my father would have yielded eventually. His categorical refusal was part of the educational system of the time. Young people were considered incapable of making their own decisions, so when they pitted their will against their parents', it had to be put to the test. When I capitulated at the first obstacle, they assumed that mine was not a true vocation but a passing whim.

For my father, and for my mother too, children were first and foremost a social duty. Intellectual and spiritual development was neglected while the most banal aspects of 'manners' were subjected to the most extreme severity. At table I had to sit up straight with my elbows tucked into my sides. If, as I did it, my thoughts were only on the best way of committing suicide, no matter. Appearance was everything; all else was unbecoming.

So I grew up with a sense of being a kind of ape that had to be well trained rather than a human being, a person capable of joy and disappointment, and needing to be loved. This deprivation soon gave rise to a great sense of loneliness, and the loneliness grew more and more profound with the years; it was a kind of vacuum in which I could only act with the slow, clumsy movements of a diver. The sense of isolation was also brought about by questions I asked myself and to which I had no answers. At the age of four or five I was already looking around and wondering, 'Why am I here, and where have all these things about me come from; what's behind it all, were they always here even before I existed, and will they continue to exist for ever?' I was asking all the questions that sensitive children ask when confronted with the complexities of the world. I believed that grown-ups asked the same questions and that they were able to answer them, but after trying to question my mother and the nanny two or three times, I realized that not only did they not know the answers but that they had never asked themselves the questions.

So my sense of isolation increased, you see. I had to resolve every problem myself, and the older I grew the more questions I asked, and the questions were always bigger, more awe-inspiring; just to think about them terrified me.

My first encounter with death came when I was six. My father had a gun-dog called Argus; he was gentle and affectionate and was my favourite playmate. I would spend whole afternoons feeding him messes of mud and grass, or sometimes I would play hairdressers and he would slope around the garden uncomplainingly, his ears bristling with hairpins. But one day, when I was in the middle of trying out a new hairdo on him, I noticed a swelling on his neck. For some weeks previously he hadn't been running and jumping about as he used to, and if I sat in a corner eating a biscuit he no longer sat in front of me sighing hopefully.

One morning when I got home from school, he was not waiting for me at the gate. At first I thought he must have gone off somewhere with my father, but when I saw my father sitting calmly in his study with no Argus curled at his feet, I was seized with a terrible foreboding. I ran out and called for him at the top of my voice all over the garden, then searched the house from top to bottom two or three times. That night, when I went to give my parents the obligatory goodnight kiss, I summoned all my courage and asked, 'Where's Argus?' 'Argus,' my father replied without looking up from his newspaper, 'has gone away.' 'Why?' I asked. 'Because he was tired of your pranks.'

Tactlessness? Superficiality? Sadism? What was behind that reply? The moment I heard it, something snapped inside me. I couldn't sleep at night, and during the day the slightest thing was enough to make me burst into tears. After a month or two a paediatrician was summoned. 'The child is exhausted,' he said, and prescribed codliver oil. Why I couldn't sleep, why I carried Argus's chewed ball with me wherever I went, no one ever asked.

That episode signalled my entry into the adult world. At six years old? Yes, at six years old. If Argus had gone away because I had been naughty, then my behaviour influenced my surroundings. It influenced them by making things disappear, by destroying them.

From that moment my actions were never neutral, never ends in themselves. Terrified of making another mistake, I reduced them bit by bit to a minimum, became apathetic, hesitant. At night I held the ball tightly in my hands and wept, saying, 'Argus, please come back, even if I did something wrong I love you more than anything else.' When my father acquired another puppy I didn't even look at it. It was, and I intended that it should remain, a complete stranger.

The rearing of children was governed by hypocrisy. I well remember an occasion when, walking with my father, I found a dead robin. With no hesitation I picked it up and showed it to him. 'Put it down,' he said immediately, 'can't you see it's sleeping?' Death, like love, was a taboo subject. Would it not have been a thousand times better if he had told me that Argus was dead? My father could have put his arms around me and said, 'He was ill, so I killed him to put an end to his suffering. He's better off where he is now.' Of course I would have cried even more, I would have been desolate for months and months, I would have gone to the place where he was buried and talked to him for hours. But, little by little, I would have begun to forget him, other things would have claimed my attention, my affection, and Argus would have slipped into the background of my mind as a memory, a sweet childhood memory. Instead, Argus became a little death that I still carry inside me.

That's why I say that I became an adult at six years old, because joy had been replaced by anxiety, curiosity by indifference. Were my parents monsters? No, definitely not; they were absolutely normal for their time.

Only in her old age did my mother begin to tell me about

her own childhood. She was quite small when her own mother died. The first child had been a boy who died of pneumonia at three years old. She was conceived immediately after this, and had the misfortune not only of being a girl but of being born on the anniversary of the boy's death. To mark this unhappy coincidence, she was dressed in the colours of mourning even before she was weaned. A great portrait in oils of her brother loomed over her cradle, reminding her, every time she opened her eyes, that she was no more than a replacement, a faded copy of something better. Can you imagine it? How could she be blamed for her coldness, for her mistakes, for her determination to keep people at a distance? Even monkeys raised in the clinical surroundings of a laboratory instead of by a real mother grow sad and lose the will to live. And if we were to dig further into the past, to find out what her mother or her mother's mother were like, I wonder what else we should discover.

Unhappiness is usually transmitted through the female line. Like certain genetic disorders, it is handed down from mother to daughter. And far from becoming weaker, it becomes more intense, ineradicable and profound. That period was very different for men, who had their profession, politics, war; their energy had outlets, was able to expand. We had none of this. For generation after generation we have been confined to the bedroom, kitchen and bathroom; behind all the thousands and thousands of steps we have walked and movements we have made we have trailed the same bitterness, the same frustration.

Have I become a feminist? No, don't worry, I am only trying to see clearly what lies behind it all.

Do you remember when we used to stand on the promontory watching the fireworks over the sea on the August bank holiday? Every now and then we saw one that didn't make it into the sky, but exploded and showered its stars prematurely. Well, whenever I think about my mother's and grandmother's lives, and the lives of many people I have known, that is the image that comes to mind: fireworks dropping to earth instead of soaring into the sky.

21 November

I once read somewhere that when Manzoni was writing *I promessi sposi*, he would get up every morning eager to return to his characters. I can't say the same of myself. Despite the length of time that has passed, it gives me no pleasure to speak about my family; my mother has remained in my memory motionless and hostile like a janissary. This morning, to try and put clear water between her and myself and between myself and my memories, I went for a walk around the garden. It had rained during the night; now the sky was clear in the west but purple clouds still loomed behind the house. I went indoors before the next lot of rain came down. A thunderstorm broke shortly afterwards, and it was so dark in the house that I had to put the lights on. I unplugged the television and refrigerator to avoid lightning damage, then got the torch, put it in my pocket and came to the kitchen to prepare for our daily session.

As soon as I sat down, however, I realized that I wasn't in the right frame of mind; perhaps there was too much static in the air, but my thoughts were darting hither and yon like so many sparks. So I got up and, with the intrepid Buck at my heels, wandered round the house without any particular purpose in mind. I went into the bedroom where I slept with your grandfather, then into the one I use nowadays (which was once your mother's), then into the long-unused dining-room, and finally into your room. As I moved from one room to another, I remembered the impression the house made on me the first time I entered it. It had been chosen not by me but by my husband Augusto, and he had moreover chosen it in haste. We needed somewhere to live and couldn't put it off any longer. It was big enough and it had a garden, and that, he reckoned, fulfilled all our requirements. From the moment we stepped inside the garden gate it struck me as being tasteless, or rather in the worst possible taste. Where colour and line were concerned, there was no one part that went with any other part. From one side it looked like a Swiss chalet, from the other, with its large round window in the middle and the stepped façade of its roof, it might even have been a Dutch house beside a canal. Seen from a distance, with its seven chimney stacks of different shapes, you knew that the only place it could exist was in the Land of Nursery Rhymes. It had been built in the twenties, but there was nothing of the twenties about it. This lack of identity worried me, and it took me years to get used to the fact that it was mine, that its walls were the context of my family life.

While I was in your room there was a flash of lightning right overhead and all the lights went out. Instead of switching on the torch, I lay down on the bed. From outside came the hiss of torrential rain, the lash of the wind; inside there was a variety of noises: creaks, little thuds, the sound of wood adjusting itself. Just for a second, as I lay there with my eyes closed, I could imagine the house as a boat, a great sailing ship ploughing across the lawn. The storm lasted nearly until lunchtime, when, from the window of your room, I noticed that two big branches had fallen off the walnut tree.

Now I'm back in the kitchen, in my battle arena. I have had a bite to eat and washed up the few plates I used. Buck is asleep at my feet, worn out by the excitement of the morning. The older he gets, the more terrified he becomes of thunderstorms, and the more difficult he finds it to settle again.

In one of those books I bought when you were at nursery school, I read that the choice of the family into which one is born is governed by the cycle of life. We have that particular father and mother because they and they alone will allow us to understand something more, to advance by one infinitesimal step. But I wondered at the time how, if this is the case, so many generations can remain static. Why, instead of an advance, should there be a retreat?

In the scientific supplement of the newspaper, I read recently that evolution may not work in the way we have always thought. According to the latest theories, change is not gradual at all. The development of a longer leg, or a beak shaped differently to enable a different food source to be tapped, does not happen millimetre by millimetre, generation after generation. It can happen very suddenly: a baby can be born quite different from its mother. This is confirmed by the skeletal remains of jawbones, hooves, skulls with different teeth. In the case of some species, intermediate forms have never been found: a grandfather has one set of characteristics, his grandson another, indicating that there was a great leap in the space of a single generation. What if this were the case with human thought processes too?

Changes accumulate on the sly, gently, gently, and then suddenly explode. All at once, someone breaks the circle, decides to be different. Destiny, heredity, upbringing, where does one begin and the other end? If you stop and think about it for a single moment, you are overwhelmed by the great mystery hidden in all this.

Shortly before I married, my father's sister (she with the spirit contacts) had my horoscope drawn up by an astrologer friend of hers. Appearing one day clutching this sheet of paper, she said, 'Here you are, this is your future.' On the paper was a geometrical sketch in which the lines from one planet to another made all kinds of angles. I remember thinking as soon as I saw it that there was no harmony, no continuity in it, only a succession of jumps, of about-turns so sharp that they seemed off balance. On the back the astrologer had written: 'A difficult path to tread. You will need to arm yourself with all the virtues if you are to follow it to the end.'

This disturbed me greatly. Up to that moment my life had seemed humdrum. Yes, there had been problems, but none, so it seemed to me, of a very serious nature, no tidal waves but only the normal ripples of adolescence. Even after growing up, as a wife and mother, widow and grandmother, I have always clung to this apparent normality. The only event out of the ordinary – if one can put it like that – was your mother's tragic death. And yet, if scrutinzed with care, that star chart did not lie. Beneath the solid, even surface, the humdrum routines of my middle-class life, there was a continual movement brought about by little ups and downs, lacerations, moments of sudden darkness and yawning chasms. During my life I have often been plunged into despair, feeling like a soldier who marks time but never leaves the one spot. Times changed, people changed, everything around me changed, but I, so it seemed to me, never moved.

The sameness, the monotony of this static march was shattered by the death of your mother. My self-respect, which had never been high, crumbled in an instant. I reasoned that if I had, up to this moment, managed to take a pace or two forward, I had now fallen back suddenly and reached the lowest point in my path. During those terrible days I was afraid that I should never be able to make the effort again, that the minimal amount of understanding I had managed to acquire up to then had been blotted out at a single stroke. Luckily, I was not left to wallow in this depressed state very long: life, with all its demands, went on.

You were my life. When you arrived – small, defence-less, with no one in the world but me – you invaded this silent, sad house with your sudden bursts of laughter, your tears. I can remember watching your big baby head oscillating between the sofa and the table, and thinking that not everything had ended. Chance, with its unforesee-able generosity, had given me another bite at the cherry.

Chance. Signora Morpurgo's husband once told me that

the word does not exist in Hebrew. To imply something in relation to its casual properties, the only word available is hazard, which is Arabic. Strange, don't you think? Strange but reassuring. Where God is present, chance has no place, not even the poor little syllable that represents it. All is ordered, regulated from on high, everything that happens to you happens for a reason. I have always envied intensely those who can embrace this vision of the world without hesitation as one of the elect. For myself, despite my efforts, I have never been able to possess that vision for more than a day or two at a time. Faced with horror or injustice, I have always recoiled; instead of justifying them with a sense of gratitude, I have always felt an urgent desire to rebel boiling up inside me.

Now, however, I am about to do something really hazardous. I am sending you a kiss. How you hate kisses! They ricochet off your shell like tennis balls. But no matter, for I am sending you this kiss whether you like it or not, and you can't do anything about it because at this very moment it is flying, light and transparent, over the sea.

I'm weary. I've re-read all I have written up to this point with a degree of anxiety. Will you understand any of it? So many thoughts are crowding my mind, jostling one another like shoppers at an end-of-season sale. I can never manage to organize my thoughts, to follow a logical line from beginning to end. I sometimes wonder if it's because I never went to university. I have read a great many books, I have been curious about many things, but always with one thought for the nappies, another for the kitchen, a third for emotions. When a botanist walks through a field picking flowers, he chooses his specimens deliberately, knowing what is of interest and what is not, selecting, discarding, establishing connections. But a holidaymaker walking through the field chooses the flowers in a different way – one because it's yellow, another because it's blue, the third for its fragrance, the fourth because it happens to be growing beside the path. I suppose my attitude to knowledge is like that. Your mother was always scolding me for it. Whenever we engaged in a discussion, I invariably gave in almost immediately. 'You have no idea how to construct an argument,' she said, 'like all middle-class people, you don't know how to defend your beliefs.'

In the same way that you are imbued with a wild, nameless restlessness, your mother was imbued with ideology. For her, the fact that I spoke about small issues instead of big ones was a source of reproach. She called me reactionary, infected by bourgeois fantasies. From her point of view I was wealthy and therefore addicted to superfluity, to luxury, and naturally evilly-inclined.

From the way she sometimes looked at me, I was convinced that had there been a people's tribunal and had she presided over it she would have sentenced me to death. I was guilty of living in a detached house with a garden instead of a tenement building in a depressed suburb. My guilt was compounded because I had inherited a small income that provided for us both. Trying to avoid the mistakes my parents had made, I listened to what she said or at least made an effort to do so. I never once ridiculed her or let her see how foreign her totalitarian ideas were to my way of thinking, though she must have sensed my misgivings about her cliché-ridden arguments all the same.

Ilaria studied at the University of Padua. She could easily have gone to Trieste but she was too intolerant to continue living with me. Every time I proposed visiting her, hostile silence was her only reply. Her studies progressed very slowly; I didn't know with whom she was sharing her lodgings, she would never tell me. Knowing her weaknesses, I was worried, especially after the student revolt in Paris in May, the occupation of the universities, the student movements. Listening to her infrequent accounts on the phone, I realized that the distance between us was growing ever greater. She was always wildly enthusiastic about something, and that something was always changing. As any mother would, I tried to understand her, but it was very difficult. All was fitful, ephemeral, there were too many new ideas, too many absolutes. Instead of using words of her own, Ilaria trotted out one slogan after another. I was anxious for her mental stability. The feeling of being part of a group sharing the same certainties, the same absolute dogmas, was reinforcing her natural arrogance to a worrying degree.

During her sixth year at university, perturbed by an unusually long silence, I got on a train and went to see her. I had never done this before during the whole time she had been in Padua. The moment when she opened the door was dreadful. Instead of greeting me, she attacked me. 'Who asked you to come?' And without even giving me time to reply, she added, 'You should have told me you were coming. I was just on my way out. I've got an important exam this morning.' As she was still wearing her nightdress, this was an obvious lie, but I pretended not to notice and said, 'Never mind, it means that I can wait till you return and we can celebrate your results together.' She actually did go out quite soon, but in such a rush that she left her books on the table.

Left alone in the flat, I did as all mothers would: I started to rummage through drawers looking for some indication, anything that could help me understand the direction her life had taken. I had no intention of spying on her, to be censorious or inquisitive. Such things have never been part of my character. I simply felt a great sense of anxiety, and the only way to put my mind at rest was to find a point of contact. Apart from handbills and pamphlets of revolutionary propaganda I found nothing, not a single letter or diary. There was a poster on her bedroom wall proclaiming: 'The family is as airy and as stimulating as a gas chamber.' That, in its way, was a clue.

When Ilaria returned soon after midday, she looked as weary as when she left. 'How did the examination go?' I asked, in the most affectionate way possible. 'The same as all the others,' she replied, adding after a pause, 'Is this why you came, to check up on me?' Determined to avoid an argument, I replied, in a quiet and conciliatory manner, that I had only one desire, which was for the two of us to speak to each other.

'Speak?' she echoed incredulously. 'And what about? Your passion for mysticism?'

'About you, Ilaria,' I said gently, trying to get her eyes to meet mine. She walked over to the window, her gaze fixed upon a weeping willow long past its best. 'I've got nothing to say, at least not to you. I don't want to waste time with personal and bourgeois gossip.' Then her eyes moved from the willow to her wristwatch and she said, 'It's late, and I've got an important meeting. You'll have to go.' I did not accede to her wish. I rose from my chair, but instead of going to the door I went over to her and took her hands in mine. 'What's happening?' I asked. 'What is it that's hurting you?' I heard her breathing quicken, and added, 'My heart aches to see you in this state. Even if you reject me as a mother, I cannot reject you as a daughter. I want to help you, but unless you meet me halfway I can do nothing.' At this point her chin began to tremble as it used to when, as a child, she was about to cry. She wrenched her hands away and turned abruptly towards the corner of the room. Her thin, shrunken body was shaken by great sobs. I stroked her hair – her head was as hot as her hands had been cold. Suddenly she turned around, threw her arms about me and hid her face on my shoulder. 'Mamma,' she said, 'I . . . I . . .'

At that precise moment the telephone rang.

'Let it ring,' I whispered into her ear.

'I can't,' she replied, drying her eyes.

When she lifted the receiver her voice was once again metallic and distant. From the short conversation I gathered that something serious had happened. And indeed, as soon as she hung up she said, 'I'm sorry, but you really will have to go now.' We went out together, and on the doorstep she allowed herself a very brief, guilty embrace. 'No one can help me,' she whispered as she hugged me. I went with her to where she had left her bicycle chained to a nearby post. Sitting on the saddle, she slipped two fingers under my necklace and said, 'The pearls, eh? They're your passport. You've never had the nerve to move without them since the day you were born!'

Despite the fact that it happened so long ago, this is the episode of your mother's life that returns to haunt me over and over again. I often think about it. Why, I ask myself, of all our shared experiences, should this be the most vivid memory? Today, while I was mulling over it for the umpteenth time, a saying popped into my mind: 'The tongue will always stray to the aching tooth.' What has that got to do with it, you may ask. It has a great deal to do with it. The reason that this episode haunts me so much is because it was the one time when I could have changed things. Your mother had burst into tears, had thrown her arms about me. At that moment a tiny crack had opened in her shell, a minute fissure through which I could have entered. Once inside, I could have done as those special nails do that are designed to expand when driven into a wall; they splay out, creating space for themselves. I could have become a fixed point in her life. To do this I needed a steady nerve. When she said I had to go, I should have stayed. I should have rented a room in a nearby hotel and knocked on her door every day, persisting until that tiny fissure became a passageway. The opportunity was there, I sensed it.

But I didn't do it. Cowardice, laziness and a false sense

of reserve made me do what she told me to do. I had hated my mother's intrusions; I wanted to be a different kind of mother, to respect her independence. The mask of freedom often conceals a lack of care, a desire not to get involved. There is a very fine line between the two, and to step over it or not is the work of an instant, a decision one either takes or does not take. Only when the time has passed do you realize how important that instant was. Only then do you feel regret, only when you realize that intrusion, not liberty, was what was required. You were there, you knew what was happening, and from this knowledge should have sprung the obligation to act. Love is no friend to the lazy. To exist in all its fullness it sometimes requires strong, precise action. Can you understand? I had clothed my cowardice and indolence in the noble vestments of liberty.

An awareness of destiny only comes with age. At your age people don't usually give it a second thought; we see everything that happens as stemming from our own will. We feel like labourers laying one stone after another to make the road we must travel. Only much later do we notice that the road is already there, someone else has built it and all we have to do is follow it. We usually make this discovery at around the age of forty, and then we begin to realize that we are not uniquely responsible for what happens. This is a dangerous moment, when a drift into suffocating fatalism is not uncommon. To see the workings of destiny in all their reality, a few more years have to go by. Towards sixty, when the road behind us is longer than the one in front, we see something we never noticed before: the road we have travelled was not straight but full of bends; at every step there was a signpost pointing in another direction; a footpath peeled off on this side, a grassy ride disappeared among the trees on that. Some of these side roads we turned into without realizing it, others we didn't even notice were there; those we passed by led we know not where, nor can we know whether they would have been better or worse in the end; but although we don't know, it rankles. We could have done a certain thing but we didn't; we went backwards instead of forwards. Do you remember playing Snakes and Ladders? Life is much the same.

As you pass by the various turnings on your way, you will encounter other lives, and whether you come to know them or not, experience them to the limit or ignore them, depends entirely upon the instantaneous choices you make. Even though you are not aware of it, your whole life and that of those close to you can hang upon your choice between continuing along a straight road or taking a side turning.

22 November

There was a change in the weather last night. The wind swung round to the east, sweeping the clouds away in a matter of hours. Before settling down to write, I took a turn round the garden. The wind was still blowing strongly, reaching right under one's clothes. Buck was in transports. He wanted to play, and trotted along beside me with a fir cone in his mouth. Weak as I am at the moment, I only managed to throw it for him once, and not very far, but it made him happy all the same. Having checked on the health of your rose, I went to commune with the walnut and cherry, my favourite trees.

Do you remember how you used to tease me when you saw me standing there stroking the trunks? 'What are you doing?' you said. 'It's not a horse's neck, you know.' And when I argued that touching a tree is no different to touching any other living being, in fact rather better, you shrugged your shoulders and walked away in irritation. Why is it better? Because when I scratch Buck's head, for instance, I feel something warm and vibrant, but behind that there is always a subtle sense of restlessness. It could be the next meal, which might be too imminent or not imminent enough, it might be a longing for you, or even the memory of a bad dream. Can you see what I mean? Where dogs are concerned, or human beings, there is always too much to think about, too many needs. Their peace and happiness depend on beings other than themselves.

It is different in the case of trees. From germination to death a tree never moves from one spot. Its roots are nearer than anything else to the heart of the earth and its crown nearer to the sky. Sap courses through it from the top to the bottom, from the bottom to the top. It expands and contracts according to the daylight. It awaits the rain, it awaits the sun, it awaits one season after another, it awaits death. None of the things which enable it to live depends upon its own will. It exists; that is all. Do you now understand why it is so satisfying to caress a tree? Because it is strong and stable, because it breathes with such long, placid, deep, deep breaths. Somewhere in the Bible it says that God has wide nostrils. I know it may seem irreverent, but every time I have tried to imagine the appearance of the Divine Being my mind has conjured up the picture of an oak tree.

There was one in the garden of my childhood home with such a thick trunk that it took two people to reach around it. I used to love being close to it even when I was only four or five. I would sit there, feeling the damp grass under my bottom, the fresh wind in my hair and on my face. I would breathe deeply and know that there was a higher order of things and that I and everything around me were part of it. Even though I knew nothing about music, something sang inside me. I couldn't tell you what kind of melody it was.

There was no particular tune, it was more like the rhythmic, powerful breathing of a bellows somewhere in the region of my heart, pulsing throughout my body and mind and giving rise to a great light that was also music. I was happy to be alive, and for me, apart from that happiness, nothing mattered.

Perhaps it will seem strange or unnatural to you that a child should have such perceptions. Unfortunately, we are used to thinking of childhood as a period of blindness, of incompleteness, not as a time of greater richness. And yet, if we look carefully at the eyes of a newborn baby, we see that it is so. Have you ever tried? Do so if you have the chance. Forget your prejudices and just observe. What is the look in those eyes? Empty, unconscious? Or is it an ancient, faraway, wise look? Babies are endowed by nature with a wider and deeper perception than adults; it is we who have lost it and cannot accept our loss. At the age of four or five I knew nothing of religion and God, or of the tight corners men have painted themselves into speaking of such things.

You know, when I had to choose if you should receive religious instruction at school or not, I thought about it for a long time. On the one hand I could remember how catastrophic my first impact with dogmas had been, on the other I was absolutely convinced that education should not only concern itself with the mind but also with the spirit. In the end the problem solved itself, the day your first hamster died. You held it in your hand and looked up at me, perplexed. 'Where is he now?' you asked. I replied by repeating your own question. 'Where do you think he is now?' Do you remember what you said? 'He's in two different places. Some of him is here, and some of him is up in the clouds.' We buried him that same afternoon with a little funeral ceremony. Kneeling in front of the little mound of earth you said a prayer: 'Be happy, Tony. One day we shall be together again.'

Perhaps I never told you, but I spent the first five years of my school life in a convent, the Institute of the Sacred Heart. The damage this did to me, with my eager, enquiring mind, was, I assure you, considerable. The sisters kept a large manger scene set up beside the main entrance to the school all year round. There was Baby Jesus in the stall with Joseph and Mary, the ox and the ass, and all around were hills and valleys of papier-mâché inhabited only by a flock of sheep. Each sheep represented a pupil and, depending on her behaviour during the day, would be moved nearer or farther away from Jesus in his stall. Every morning we passed by this before going to our classrooms, and as we did so we were obliged to observe our positions. On the side opposite the stable was a deep, deep chasm, and it was here that the naughtiest children were placed with two legs dangling in midair. Between the ages of six and ten my life was conditioned by the movements of my lamb. And I need hardly tell you that it seldom moved from the lip of the precipice.

Inside me, I tried so hard to respect the rules I had been taught, partly from a child's natural sense of conformity but also because I truly felt that one should be good, that one should not tell lies or be vain. Nevertheless, I was always about to topple over the edge. Why? For silly little things. When I went to the mother superior in tears and asked her to tell me why I had been moved yet again, she replied, 'Because you had too big a bow in your hair yesterday', or 'Because one of your classmates heard you singing as you left the school,' or 'Because you didn't wash your hands before dinner.' You see? Once again my misdemeanours were external, just like those of which my mother accused me. What I was being taught was not inner harmony but outward conformity. One day, teetering on the very edge of the chasm, I burst into tears, protesting, 'But I love Jesus.' And do you know what the nun standing beside me said? 'Ah, so you are a liar as well as being untidy. If you really loved Jesus you would keep your copy books tidier.' And with a flick of her finger she sent my sheep hurtling into the abyss.

I believe it was two whole months after that episode before I could sleep. Whenever I closed my eyes the mattress beneath me became a sea of flames and horrible voices sneered at me behind my back, saying, 'Just you wait, we're coming to get you!' Naturally, I said nothing about all this to my parents. Seeing me pale-faced and tense, my mother decided that I had been overdoing things and I had to swallow spoonful after spoonful of tonic.

I wonder how many sensitive, intelligent people have turned their backs permanently on spiritual things as the result of such an episode. Every time I hear someone say how much they enjoyed their schooldays and wish they could have them over again, I am perplexed. For me it was one of the worst periods in my life, possibly the worst of all given the dominating sense of impotence. Throughout my elementary schooling I was torn violently between the desire to be faithful to what I felt inside me and the wish to comply with what other people believed even though I instinctively felt it to be false.

It's strange, but as I relive now the emotions of that period, I have the impression that for me the great crisis of growing up happened not during adolescence, as it usually does, but during those years of early childhood. By the time I was twelve, thirteen, fourteen, I had already reached a sad kind of maturity. The great metaphysical questions had gradually lost their urgency and been replaced by new and harmless fantasies. I went to church with my mother on Sundays and the compulsory holy days, but while I knelt demurely to accept the communion bread my mind was on other things; this was no more than one of the little performances necessary for a quiet life. That's why I did not enrol you for religious instruction, nor have I ever regretted my decision. When you, with childish curiosity, asked me questions on the subject, I tried to reply in as open and direct a way as possible, respecting the sense of mystery that we all possess. And when your questions ceased I made a tactical withdrawal and never raised the subject again. This is an area in which silence is golden; otherwise the same thing can happen that happens to travelling salesmen. The more they push their product, the more you suspect them of trying to sell you a pup. With you, I only sought to avoid quenching what was there. For the rest I waited.

You mustn't run away with the idea that my path was

always smooth, however. Although at the age of six I was alive to the heartbeat at the centre of things, by the age of seven I had forgotten all about it. To begin with, certainly, I still heard the music; it was muted, but still there. It was like a stream flowing through a mountain gorge which I could hear, if I stood still and listened, from the edge of the overhanging cliff. Later, the mountain stream changed into an old radio, a radio on its last legs. At one moment the song burst from it too loud for comfort, the next moment it was silent.

My father and mother never wasted an opportunity to scold me for my habit of singing. Once, during a meal, my father actually slapped my face – the first time I'd ever been slapped in my life – because I had unconsciously burbled a few notes. 'We don't sing at table,' he thundered. 'Only singers are allowed to sing,' said my mother, following his lead. 'But I've got something inside me that sings,' I protested. Anything that was not part of the material world was incomprehensible to my parents. So what chance did I have of holding on to my music? Had I been destined for sainthood, perhaps I could have saved it. But my destiny was the cruel one of normality.

Little by little the music faded into silence, and with it went the profound sense of joy that had been with me in my first years. The loss of joy, I must say, is the thing I have mourned more than any other. Later, indeed, I felt happiness, but happiness is to joy as an electric light-bulb is to the sun. Happiness is always caused by something; you are happy *about* something, it is a feeling that comes from the outside. Joy, on the other hand, is not caused by anything. It possesses you for no apparent reason; it is essentially rather like the sun, which gives off heat thanks to the combustion of its own core.

Over the years I abandoned my self, the deepest part of me, to become another person, the person my parents wanted me to be. I exchanged my personality for a character. Character, as you will find out for yourself, is valued much more highly than personality.

Character and personality, contrary to what you might believe, are not the same thing, indeed one excludes the other in most instances. My mother, for example, had a strong character, she was sure of herself in everything she did and there was nothing, absolutely nothing, that could shake this. I was her exact opposite. In daily life there was nothing that sent me into ecstasies. When required to make a decision I vacillated and put it off for so long that those around me eventually lost patience and made the decision for me.

Don't think that putting aside my personality and adopting a synthetic character was easy for me. Deep down something continued to rebel against the process. Part of me wanted to go on being myself, while the other part, in order to be loved, wanted to conform to other people's expectations. What a gruelling battle! I detested my mother with her superficial, empty manner. I detested her and yet slowly, against my will, I began to resemble her. This is the high and terrible price of upbringing, a price it is almost impossible to avoid paying. No child can live without love, so we try to conform to the model we are given even if we dislike it and think it wrong. Nor does the effect of this psychological process disappear when we are grown up. As soon as you are a mother it surfaces without your realizing it or wanting it and conditions your actions once more. When your mother was born I was convinced that I would act in a different way. And in effect I did. To avoid imposing a model upon your mother, as had happened to me, I left her free to make her own choices, I wanted her to feel that she had my approval for everything she did, and was always telling her, 'We are two different people and can respect each other even while we agree to differ.'

There was a flaw in this, a major flaw. Do you know what that was? It was my lack of self-assurance, of identity. Even though I was an adult I was sure of nothing. I had no self-love, no self-respect. Your mother, with the subtle, opportunistic sensitivity of a child, realized this almost immediately. She perceived my weakness, my insecurity, my spinelessness. When I think about our relationship, the image that comes to mind is that of a tree with a parasitic climber. The tree is older, taller, has been there for a long time and has deeper roots. The climber growing at its feet has sprung up in a single season; it has barbs and tendrils rather than roots, and under each tendril are tiny suckers with which it clings to the bark. In one or two years it reaches the crown of the tree. When the host sheds its leaves, the parasite remains green. It continues to spread, to develop more and more aerial roots, until the tree is completely covered and only the parasite has access to sunlight and water. The tree then dries up and dies, only the poor starved trunk remaining as a support for the creeper.

After her tragic death I thought no more about her for several years. Sometimes it occurred to me that I had forgotten her and I would accuse myself of heartlessness. True, I had you to look after, but I don't think that was the real reason, or maybe it was partly. My sense of defeat was too bitter to be acknowledged. Only in the last few years, when you were growing apart from me and beginning to strike out on your own path, have I begun to think about your mother again, to the point of obsession. My greatest regret is that I was never brave enough to stand up to her, to tell her that she was wrong, that she was about to do something stupid. I heard her come out with extremely dangerous slogans which, in her own interests, I should have contradicted, but I failed to intervene. This was not a case of idolence. The subjects we discussed were of vital importance. The reason for my action – or rather my inaction – was my mother's attitude. In order to be loved, I had to avoid disputes and pretend to be something I was not. Ilaria was naturally overbearing, she had more character than me and I was afraid of open disagreements. Had I really loved her I would have got angry, I would have been firm with her, I would have insisted on her doing or not doing certain things. Perhaps this was what she really wanted, what she needed.

I wonder why the simple truths are the most difficult to understand? Had I understood at the time that the first requirement of love is strength, events would most likely have taken a different turn. But to be strong you must have self-respect; and to have self-respect you must have self-knowledge, must know yourself inside out, even the most hidden things, those most difficult to accept. How can one achieve this when life with all its noise and bustle is always dragging one forward? Only those with very special gifts can even attempt it. Ordinary mortals like me and your mother have no choice but to accept the fate that overtakes dead branches and plastic bottles hurled by someone – or blown by the wind, perhaps – into a river. Thanks to the material of which you are made you float instead of sinking; you notch this up as a victory and immediately begin to travel; you slip quickly down on the current; every now and then you find yourself caught in a tangle of roots or a hump of stones; you stay there for a while, battered by the water, then the level rises and you float free to continue on your way; while the water flows smoothly you stay on the surface, when it is churned by the rapids you go under; you don't know where you are bound, nor have you ever wondered about it; along the quieter stretches you can observe the landscape, the banks, the bushes; you see shapes and colours rather than details, you are moving too quickly to see more; then, as time and the miles slip by, the banks become lower, the river wider, still in a channel but not for much longer. 'Where am I going?' you wonder, and in that instant you see the ocean before you.

Most of my life has been like this. I have thrashed around rather than swum. With uncertain, uncoordinated movements, without elegance or joy, I have just managed to keep afloat.

Why am I telling you all this? What significance have these long, over-intimate confessions? Perhaps by now you are already bored, puffing with annoyance as you skim through page after page. What is she getting at, you will be wondering, and where does it leave me? True, I do get distracted and, instead of always following the high road, willingly turn off into narrow by-ways. I give the impression of getting lost; perhaps it is not an impression at all, and I really am lost. But this is the path that must be followed to reach what you seek so longingly: the centre.

Do you remember my showing you how to cook pancakes? When you toss them, I said, think about anything except catching them neatly in the pan. If you think too hard about them when they're in the air, you can be sure they will land in a crumpled heap. It sounds mad, but distraction really is the secret of arriving at the centre of things, at their very heart.

It's not so much my heart as my stomach that is now making itself felt. It is rumbling, and quite right too, because what with pancakes and trips down the river, supper time is here. Now I must stop, but before I do so I send you another of those kisses you hate.

29 November

Yesterday's wind claimed a victim, as I found this morning on my usual turn around the garden. My guardian angel must have been watching over me, for instead of just walking round the house as I usually do, I went down to the far end, to the place where the chicken-run used to be and where the compost heap is now. Just as I was walking along beside the wall separating our garden from Walter's, I noticed something dark on the ground. It could almost have been a pine cone, but it wasn't because it was moving at more or less regular intervals. I had gone out without my glasses, and it was only when I was actually standing over it that I saw that it was a young blackbird, a female. I nearly broke a leg trying to catch it because it kept hopping away just as I was about to reach it. Had I been younger I could have got hold of it in less than a second, but I move too slowly now. In the end I had a brainwave. I took off my headscarf and threw it over the bird. Then I picked the whole bundle up, carried it into the house and put the tiny creature into an old shoe box lined with rags, making holes in the lid, one big enough for her to poke her head through.

As I write she's on the table in front of me, but I haven't

given her anything to eat yet because she's too agitated. Seeing the bird agitated makes me agitated too, and the fear in her eyes makes me uneasy. If a fairy were to come down right now, appearing in a blinding flash between the fridge and the cooker, do you know what I would wish for? King Solomon's ring, the magic ring that makes it possible to speak to any animal in the world. Then I could tell the blackbird, 'Don't be afraid, my little chickabiddy, I may be a human being but I have the best of intentions. I'll look after you, I'll feed you and when you are better again I'll set you free.'

But let's get back to talking about us. Yesterday we parted in the kitchen after my homely parable of the pancakes. This will almost certainly have irritated you. Young people always assume that serious subjects demand serious, highfalutin words. Shortly before you left you put a letter under my pillow in which you tried to explain your problems. Now that you are far away I can admit that – apart from your state of disquiet – I understood not a word of it. Everything was convoluted, obscure. I'm a simple person, I belong to an epoch very different from yours: I call a spade a spade. Problems can only be resolved in the light of everday experience, from seeing things as they are and not how someone else thinks they should be. As soon as we throw the ballast overboard, discarding whatever does not belong to us, that which comes from outside, we are on the right track. I have so often had the impression that the books you read confuse rather than enlighten you, that they leave a black cloud around you like the ink ejected by a squid escaping from a predator.

Before you decided to leave, you offered me a choice: I could either let you go away for a year or I could send you to a psychiatrist. My reaction was uncompromising, remember? You can go away for three years if you like, I said, but to a psychiatrist you will never go. Not once. I should not allow it even if you paid for it yourself. You were taken aback by such an extreme reaction. The truth of the matter was that you believed you were offering me a lesser evil. Although you never said as much, I imagine you reckoned that I was too old or too ill-informed to understand such things. You were wrong. Even as a child I had heard people speak about Freud. One of my father's brothers was a doctor who, having studied in Vienna, came into contact with his theories very early on. He was enthusiastic about them and tried to convince my parents about their effectiveness whenever he came to dinner. 'You will never convince me that if I dream about spaghetti it means that I am afraid of death,' my mother would snort. 'If I dream about spaghetti it means that I am hungry, nothing more.' My uncle tried in vain to convince her that her stubborn resistance was due to ignorance of Freud's theory of displacement, but that her terror of death was indisputable because spaghetti and worms were demonstrably the same thing and worms were what we should all become one day. And do you know what my mother said? After a short, silent pause, she piped up in her soprano voice, 'So what if I dream about macaroni?'

My encounters with psychoanalysis are not, however,

limited to this childhood episode. Your mother went to a psychoanalyst – so-called – for nearly ten years; she was still going to him when she died, so I was able to observe the whole development of the relationship, day after day, though admittedly at one remove. In the beginning, true, she told me nothing about it. As you know, such things are the subject of professional confidentiality. What struck me immediately, however, and in a very negative way, was the instantaneous and total sense of dependency. After no more than a month, her entire life revolved around those appointments and what happened during them between herself and that man. Jealousy, you'll say. Maybe. That could have come into it, but it was never the main factor; what distressed me was to see her in total subjection to yet another influence; first it had been politics, now this man. Ilaria had got to know him during her last year in Padua, and it was to Padua that she went every week. When she told me about this new activity I was perplexed to begin with, and asked her if it was really necessary to go so far afield to find a decent doctor.

In one way her decision to seek medical advice for her stressed condition was a relief to me, for I thought seeking help was itself a step in the right direction. On the other hand, however, knowing her weakness I was worried about her choice of person to trust. Dealing with someone else's mind is always a matter of extreme delicacy. 'How did you find him?' I asked. 'Did someone recommend him to you?' But she only shrugged her shoulders and said, 'You wouldn't understand.' And shut up like a clam.

Although we each had our own homes in Trieste, we

were in the habit of having a meal together at least once a week. Our mealtime conversations, from the time when she began her psychotherapy, were entirely and deliberately superficial. We chatted about what was happening in the city, or the weather. When the weather was fine and nothing was happening in the city, we ate in almost total silence.

But even after her third or fourth trip to Padua, I noticed a change. Instead of neither of us talking, she began to ask questions. She wanted to know all about the past, about me, her father, our relationship. There was neither affection nor curiosity in her questions; I felt as if I were being interrogated. She would ask the same question several times, insisting on the most minute details, casting doubts on incidents involving herself which she remembered perfectly well. I felt at such times as if I were talking not to my own daughter but to a police officer who, come what may, would make me confess to some crime. One day, my patience exhausted, I said, 'Be honest with me. Tell me what you are really trying to get at.' She gave me an ironic look, picked up a fork, tapped it on her glass, and when the glass went *ping* she replied, 'Only one thing: the truth. I want to know when and why you and your husband clipped my wings.'

That was the last time I allowed myself to be subjected to a similar barrage of questions. The very next week when I phoned her I told her that she was more than welcome to come for lunch, but on one condition, that instead of cross-examination there should be dialogue between us.

Did I have an Achilles' heel? I did indeed, for while there

were many things I enjoyed discussing with Ilaria, I thought it neither right nor healthy to reveal such intimate matters under the pressure of interrogation. Had I continued to play her game, we would not have entered upon a new, adult relationship; I should have been merely – and for ever – the guilty party and she would have been for ever the victim, with no possibility of change for the better.

Several months later I spoke to her again about her therapy. By now she was engaging in sessions with her doctor lasting for a whole weekend at a time. She had lost a lot of weight and there was an edge of hysteria in her speech that I had never previously heard. I told her about her great-uncle, about his first encounters with psychoanalysis, and then asked her, as if it were a matter of no importance, 'To which school does your analyst belong?' 'He doesn't belong to any school,' she replied, 'or rather, to one he founded himself.'

From that moment, what had been simple concern became a matter of genuine anxiety. I managed to discover the name of the doctor and a few enquiries elicited the fact that he had no medical qualifications at all. The hopes I had cherished about the effectiveness of the therapy were dashed at a blow. It was not, of course, the mere absence of a degree that made me suspicious, but the absence of a degree coupled with the fact that Ilaria's condition was steadily deteriorating. If this were a valid course of therapy, I argued, a difficult phase at the beginning would have been followed by an improvement; slowly, despite doubts and setbacks along the way, a new awareness would have begun to make itself felt. Instead of which, Ilaria was slowly losing interest in everything around her. She had finished her studies several years before, yet she was still doing nothing; she had lost touch with the few friends she used to have and her only occupation was scrutinizing her mental processes with the obsessive interest of an entomologist. The world revolved around what she had dreamt the night before or a phrase uttered by me or her father twenty years ago. Watching her quality of life deteriorating in this way, I felt quite impotent.

Three years later, in the summer, there was a glimmer of hope that lasted for a few weeks. Shortly after Easter I suggested we go on holiday together. To my great surprise, instead of rejecting the idea out of hand, Ilaria looked up from her plate and asked, 'Where could we go?' 'I don't know,' I replied, 'wherever you like, or where the fancy takes us.'

That very afternoon we could hardly wait for the travel agencies to open. For weeks we beat a path to their doors trying to find a place we liked the look of. In the end we plumped for Greece – Crete and Santorini – at the end of May. Preparations for the trip brought us closer than we had ever been before. She was obsessed with packing, terrified of leaving the most important things behind. To calm her down I bought a little notebook and told her to make a list of all the things she needed and cross them off as she put them in the suitcase.

That evening, as I got ready for bed, I reproached myself for not having realized earlier that a trip together would be one of the best ways of trying to repair our relationship.

Then the Friday before we were due to leave, Ilaria phoned me. Her voice sounded hard. I believe she was in a public phone-box. 'I've got to go to Padua,' she said, 'but I'll be back Thursday evening at the latest.' 'Do you really have to go?' I asked. But she had already hung up.

I heard nothing from her until the following Thursday when the phone rang at two o'clock. Her tone was a mixture of hardness and regret. 'I'm sorry,' she said, 'but I'm not coming to Greece.' She waited for my reaction; I waited for her to continue. After a few seconds I replied, 'I am also very sorry. But I shall go all the same.' She understood my disappointment and tried to make excuses. 'If I go I shall only be running away from myself,' she whispered.

As you can imagine, it was a miserable holiday. I forced myself to listen to the guides, to take an interest in the landscape and the archaeological sites, but all the time I was thinking only of your mother and wondering where her life was leading her.

Ilaria, I told myself, is like a gardener who having planted his seeds and watched the first little spikes appear is seized with fear lest something harm them. So, to protect them from wind and rain, he buys a fine sheet of plastic and covers them over; to keep off the greenfly and caterpillars he sprays them with hefty doses of insecticide. He has to work incessantly, there's no moment of the day or night when he is not thinking about his plants and how to protect them. Then one morning, lifting the plastic sheeting, he discovers to his surprise and sorrow that they have all rotted and died. Had he left them to grow freely, some would have died, but some would have survived. Carried by the wind and by insects, other seeds would have sprung up beside the ones he sowed; some would have been weeds that he would have had to pull up, but others would have become flowers whose colours would have cheered up an otherwise dreary kitchen garden. Do you see what I'm driving at? This is how things are; life demands generosity; if we cultivate our own little character regardless of the things around us, we continue to breathe but we are dead.

By imposing an excessive rigidity upon her mind, Ilaria had suppressed the voice of her heart – a word which, as the result of discussions with her, I used only with fear and trembling. Once, when she was in her teens, I said, 'The heart is the power-house of the spirit.' The next morning I found the dictionary open on the kitchen table at the word spirit; the definition had been underlined in red: 'colourless liquid used to conserve fruit'.

These days the word 'heart' has only naïve, even vulgar, associations. When I was young one could still use the word without embarrassment, but nowadays nobody uses it at all. On the rare occasions when you do hear the word it is only with reference to some malfunction, and what is implied is not 'heart' in the fullness of its meaning but a medical condition. No one so much as hints at the heart's role as the core of the human soul. I have often asked myself the reason for such ostracism. Augusto often used to say, quoting the Bible: 'He who puts his trust in his own heart is a fool.' Why on earth should he be a fool? Could it be because the heart bears some resemblance to a combustion chamber? Because there is darkness there, darkness and fire? The mind is as modern as the heart is ancient. Those who listen to their hearts – so people seem to think nowadays – are closer to the animals, to the irrational, while those who listen to the voice of reason are closer to higher things. But supposing this were not so, that the exact opposite were the truth? Could excess of ratiocination be impoverishing our lives?

On the ship coming back from Greece I got into the habit of spending some time near the bridge every morning. I enjoyed peering into it and seeing the radar and the complicated instrumentation that tells us where we are going. One day, while I was watching the different antennae quivering in the wind, it occurred to me that people are becoming more and more like radios that can only pick up one frequency. Rather like those tiny radios given away as advertising gimmicks: every station is marked on the dial, but twiddling the knob will produce sounds from only one or two while all the others hum unheard in the ether. In my opinion using the mind too much produces the same effect: out of all the reality that surrounds us we can pick up only a limited amount. And even this is often confused because it is stuffed with words and the words, more often than not, lead us round in circles rather than into a wider space.

Understanding requires silence. As a young woman I didn't know that, but I do now that I find myself rambling through the house as silent and solitary as a goldfish in a bowl. It's a bit like attacking a dirty floor with a broom or a wet cloth. If you use a broom most of the dust rises into the air and resettles all over the place, but if you use a wet cloth the floor will be clean and shiny. Silence is like a wet cloth: it does away for ever with the film of dust. Words imprison the mind, and if they have any rhythm at all it is that of disjointed thoughts. The heart, on the other hand, is more restful. It is the only organ that beats, and its pulsation puts us in tune with greater pulsations. It happens occasionally that I leave the television on all afternoon – usually out of absentmindedness – and even though I'm not watching it I can hear it all over the house. By the time I go to bed I'm more tense than usual and find it hard to get to sleep. Continuous noise and bustle are a kind of drug, and once you have acquired the habit you can't do without it.

I don't want to add much more for now. The pages I have written today put me in mind of a cake prepared from several different recipes and containing a wild assortment of almonds, cream cheese, raisins, rum, sponge fingers, marzipan, chocolate and strawberries – in fact one of those dreadful concoctions you once made me try, telling me that it was 'nouvelle cuisine'. A jumble? Maybe. If a philosopher read it, I can imagine he would be unable to restrain himself from making red marks all over it as the old teachers used to do. 'Inconsistent,' he would write, 'not to the point, logically untenable.'

Just imagine what a psychologist would make of it! He could write a whole monograph on the failure of relations with my daughter and about all that I omitted to do or say. But even if I have omitted some things, is it important any more? I had a daughter and I lost her. She died in a car crash: that very day I had told her that the father who (according to her) had made her life miserable, was not her real father. I can remember every moment of that day as clearly as if I were watching a film, except that the film is nailed to the wall instead of being fed through a projector. I know the sequence of scenes by heart, and every detail of every scene. I have forgotten nothing, it is all inside me, pulsing in my mind whether I wake or sleep. It will pulse even after my death.

The baby blackbird has woken up and keeps popping her head through the hole in the box and making a determined little cheep at regular intervals. She seems to be saying, 'I'm hungry! Why aren't you feeding me?' I got up just now and had a look in the fridge to see if there was anything suitable; there wasn't so I rang Walter to ask if he had any worms he could let me have. While I was dialling I told the blackbird, 'You don't know how lucky you are to have hatched from an egg and to have forgotten, after your first flight, what your parents looked like.'

30 November

Shortly before nine o'clock this morning, Walter arrived with his wife and a little bag of worms, mealworms provided by a cousin who goes fishing. With his help I lifted the blackbird very gently out of the box; beneath the soft breast feathers the tiny heart was beating like a mad thing. I took the worms from the plate with metal tweezers and offered them to the chick, but however much I waved them in front of her beak, she took no notice at all. 'Open it with a toothpick,' suggested Walter, 'or force it open with your fingers.' But I, naturally, didn't have the nerve. Then, remembering all those baby birds that you and I reared together, I recalled how we had learned to stroke the side of the beak. And, indeed, as soon as I did this the blackbird's beak flew open as if I had touched a spring. After only three worms it had had enough. Signora Razman made some coffee – something I haven't been able to do since my arm got so weak – and we sat down and chatted for a while. My life would have been so much more difficult lately without their kindness and helpfulness. In a few days' time they are planning a visit to the nursery to buy bulbs and seeds ready for next spring. They asked me to go with them, but I said I'd think about it and phone them at nine tomorrow morning.

It was the eighth of May. I had been working in the garden all morning. The aquilegias were in flower and the cherry tree was still covered with blossom. Completely unexpectedly, your mother turned up at lunchtime. She crept up behind me silently, then suddenly shouted, 'Surprise, surprise!' I was so startled I dropped the rake. This enthusiasm and affected jollity were belied by the expression on her face, which was white, her lips compressed. She kept running her fingers through her hair as she spoke, flicking it away from her face, tugging it, putting an end in her mouth.

For some time, this had been her habitual state, so I was not unduly worried, at least not more than usual. I asked her where you were. She told me she had left you playing at a friend's house. As we walked towards the house, she pulled a bedraggled bunch of forget-me-nots from her pocket. 'It's Mother Day,' she said, and stood there, apparently rooted to the ground. So I took the initiative, went to her, gave her an affectionate hug and thanked her. The feel of her body against mine was a shock. There was a dreadful rigidity about it, and it became even stiffer as I embraced her. I had the strange sensation that her body was hollow; it gave off a chill like a cave. I remember so clearly that I thought about you immediately. What will happen to that child, I wondered, with a mother reduced to such a state? The situation was getting worse rather than better, and I was worried about you, about your development. Your mother was very possessive and brought you to see me as seldom as she could. She wanted to protect you from my negative influence. I had spoilt her life and was not to be allowed to spoil yours.

It was lunchtime, and after our little hug I went to the kitchen to prepare some food. As the weather was mild we set the table outside, under the wisteria. I used the green-and-white checked cloth and put the forget-me-nots in a little vase in the middle of the table. You see? I remember everything with incredible clarity, given my unreliable memory. Did I have a presentiment that this was the last time I would see her alive? Or has my memory played tricks on me, since the tragedy, by embroidering the truth about the time we spent together? Who can tell? Not I.

As there was no food prepared, I made a tomato sauce and when it was nearly ready I asked Ilaria what kind of pasta she would like. She called 'I don't mind' from the garden, so I used fusilli. When we were sitting down I asked some questions about you, to which she replied evasively. The air around us was alive with insects; they were flying in and out of the flowers and buzzing so loudly that at times it was difficult to hear what the other was saying. Suddenly a black something plopped on to your mother's plate. 'It's a wasp! Kill it! Kill it!' she shouted, leaping from her chair and upsetting everything. I leant over to look, saw that it was a bumblebee and told her, 'It's not a wasp, it's a bumblebee, it's harmless.' Having shooed it away from the table, I put the pasta back in her plate. She sat down again, still looking shaken, picked up her fork, fiddled with it for a while, passing it from one hand to the other, then leant her elbows on the table and said, 'I need some money.' On the tablecloth, where the fusilli had fallen, was a large red stain.

This question of money had already been going on for some months. Even before Christmas the year before, Ilaria had admitted signing some papers in favour of her analyst, but when I asked for clarification, she had ducked the question as always. 'Only guarantees,' she had said, 'a mere formality.' This was her way of terrorizing me. When she had something to tell me, she would only tell me half of it. She unloaded her anxiety on to me, and having done so refused to tell me facts that would have put me in a position to help her. There was a subtle sadism in all this and also a burning need to be the object of anxiety. Usually, however, she was only trying it on. She once said, for example, 'I've got cancer of the ovaries,' and after brief but laborious enquiries I discovered that she had simply had a routine examination: the same smear test every woman has. Do you see? It was a bit like the boy who cried wolf, for over the last few years she had told me about so many imminent tragedies that in the end I ceased to believe them, or rather, to take them seriously. So when she told me about signing these papers I didn't pay much attention and didn't insist on more information. Apart from anything else, I was tired of her wearisome games. And even if I had insisted, even if I had known about it earlier, it would have done no good as she had already signed the papers some time previously without asking my advice.

The real crisis came at the end of February, when I learnt for the first time that the documents Ilaria had signed underwrote the business of her doctor to the tune of three hundred million lire. Within those two months the society for whom she had signed the surety had gone bankrupt, there was a shortfall of nearly two billion and the banks had begun to call in the debts. At that point your mother came crying to me, asking me what on earth she was to do. The collateral she had put up for the guarantee was the house in which the two of you lived, and the banks now wanted that back. You can imagine how furious I was. At over thirty years of age your mother was not only completely incapable of supporting herself without my help but she had put at risk the only possession she had – the flat I put in her name when you were born. I was beside myself, but I didn't let her see this. To avoid putting more pressure on her, I feigned calm and simply said, 'We'll see what can be done.'

As she had retreated into total apathy, I sought out a good lawyer. Sleuthlike, I collected every scrap of information that would strengthen our hand when dealing with the banks. And thus it was that I stumbled upon the fact that for several years her analyst had been giving her powerful drugs. If she was depressed during a session, he offered her whisky. He repeated over and over again that she was his favourite and most gifted pupil, and that she would soon be in a position to set up her own practice and treat other people. Just to repeat these words sends shivers down my spine. Just imagine Ilaria, with her weakness, her confusion, her complete lack of identity, being in a position to treat other people! Had the financial crisis not intervened, this would almost certainly have happened. Without telling me anything, she would have set herself up in the same business as her guru.

Naturally, she had never dared to say anything explicit to me about this plan of hers. Whenever I asked her why she made no use of her degree in literature, she would reply with a knowing little smile, 'You'll see, I will make use of it . . .'

Some things are very painful to think about; to speak about them is even more painful. During those dreadful months I came to understand one thing about her, something that had never remotely occurred to me before and that I do not even know if I should tell you; however, I have decided to conceal nothing from you, to tell all, so . . . You see, I had realized, quite suddenly, that your mother's intelligence was very limited. It cost me a great deal of effort to understand this and to accept it, partly because we always deceive ourselves about our own children and partly because she had managed to pull the wool over my eyes very successfully with her pretended knowledge and glib arguments. Had I been brave enough to face up to this earlier, I would have protected her better, shown more firmness in my love. Had I protected her, I might have saved her.

There was nothing more crucial than this, yet by the time it dawned on me there was almost nothing I could do. Taking the situation as a whole, there was only one sensible course of action, which was to declare her incapable of looking after her affairs and to institute proceedings for undue influence. When I told your mother that the lawyer and I had decided to do this, she became hysterical. 'You're doing this on purpose,' she shouted. 'It's all a plot to take the child away from me.' But I am sure that the thought uppermost in her mind was that if she were declared incapable, it would put paid to her career once and for all. She was teetering blindfold on the edge of a precipice and still believed she was picnicking in the fields. After the crisis she ordered me to dismiss the lawyer and not intervene further. She consulted another on her own initiative and I heard no more from her until the day she arrived with the bunch of forget-me-nots.

Can you imagine how I felt when she planted her elbows on the table and asked for money? Yes, I do appreciate that I am speaking about your mother, and perhaps you hear nothing but cold cruelty in my words and think she had every reason to hate me. But remember what I told you at the start – your mother was my daughter; I lost much more than you did. You are innocent of her fate, I am certainly not. If from time to time you think I sound detached, try to imagine the depth of my grief, a depth beyond words. The detachment is only apparent; it supplies the vacuum that allows me to speak of these things.

When she asked me to pay off her debts, for the first time in my life I said no, absolutely not. 'I'm not a Swiss bank,' I said. 'I do not possess such a sum. Even if I had, I wouldn't give it to you. You're old enough to be responsible for your own actions. I had only the one property and I made it over to you. The fact that you have lost it is nothing to do with me.' At that point she began to whimper. She began a sentence, left it in mid-air and began another. Neither the words nor the disjointed phrases seemed to make any sense, to have any logic in them. After whining for ten minutes she returned to her *idée fixe*, her father and his presumed ill-treatment of her, primarily by paying her so little attention. 'I want compensation, can't you understand?' she shouted at me, her eyes glittering horribly. Then, I don't know how, I exploded. The secret I had sworn to carry to my grave rose to my lips. As soon as the words were out I wanted to recall them, I would have done anything to swallow them, but it was too late. The statement 'Your father was not your real father' had already reached her ears. Her face became even paler. She got slowly to her feet, her eyes never leaving mine. 'What did you say?' she whispered, almost inaudibly. Strangely enough, I was now calm again. 'You heard right,' I replied. 'I said that my husband was not your father.'

Ilaria's reaction? She simply walked away. She turned, moving more like a robot than a human being, and walked towards the garden gate. 'Wait! let's talk about it!' I shouted after her in a voice that sounded dreadfully shrill.

Why didn't I get up, why didn't I run after her, why did I do nothing at all to stop her? Because I too had been petrified by the words I had spoken. Try to understand. The secret I had kept, and kept with such tenacity, for so many years, had suddenly and involuntarily escaped. In less than a second, like a canary that finds its cage door open, it had flown out and reached the one person it never should have reached.

That same afternoon, at six o'clock, while I was watering the hydrangeas, still very troubled, a patrol of traffic police arrived to tell me there had been an accident.

It's now late evening. I had to pause for a while. I fed Buck and the blackbird, I had my supper and watched a little television. My shell is too splintered to allow me to bear strong emotion for long at a time. I have to distract myself, get my breath back before continuing.

As you know, your mother was not killed outright. For ten days she hovered between life and death. I never left her during this time, hoping that she would at least open her eyes for a moment, that she would give me one last chance to ask her forgiveness. We were alone in a room full of machines, one small screen confirmed that her heart was still beating, another that her brain was almost dead. The doctor looking after her told me that patients in that state can often benefit from hearing a sound they have loved, so I managed to get a tape of the song that had been her favourite as a child and played it to her by the hour on a miserable little machine. She must have been able to hear something, because after the first few notes her face relaxed and her lips began to move like a baby's when it has finished sucking. It looked like a smile of satisfaction. Who knows, maybe a memory of untroubled times lurked in that fraction of her brain that was still active and it was there that she found comfort. The minute change filled me with joy. One grasps at straws in such a situation; I never tired of stroking her head and repeating, over and over, 'Darling, you must pull through, we've got a whole life before us to live together, we'll start again and do things differently.' While I spoke, a picture sprang into my mind. She was four or five years old and I could see her walking around the garden holding her favourite doll by one arm and talking to it non-stop. I was in the kitchen, so I couldn't hear what she was saying, but every now and then I could hear her laughing, and it was a full-blooded, joyous laugh. She was happy once, I told myself; she can be happy again. For her to be reborn we must start from that point, from that child.

Of course, the first thing the doctors told me after the accident was that even if she survived she would never be the same again. She might be paralysed or permanently brain-damaged. And do you know something? In my maternal egoism the only thing that mattered to me was that she should live. How was of no importance. On the contrary, to push her about in a wheelchair, wash her, spoonfeed her, to make caring for her the only purpose of my life, would have been the best way to expiate my guilt. Had my love been real, had I loved her from my heart, I would have prayed for her death. In the end Someone showed He loved her more than I did. In the late afternoon of the ninth day, the little smile faded from her lips and she died. I realized at once what had happened, but didn't tell the nurse right away because I wanted to stay with her a little longer. I stroked her face, squeezed her hands as I had done when she was little, and continued to whisper, 'My darling, my darling.' Then, without releasing her hand, I knelt at the foot of the bed and began to pray. And as I prayed, the tears began to flow.

When the nurse tapped me on the shoulder I was still weeping. 'Come with me,' she said, 'and I'll give you a sedative.' I refused the sedative; I didn't want anything to lessen my grief. I stayed there until they took her to the mortuary. Then I got a cab and went to the house of my friend who was looking after you. That same evening you were at home with me. 'Where's Mummy?' you asked while we were having supper. 'Mummy has gone on a journey,' I said, 'a long journey right up into the sky.' You went on eating, your big blonde head bowed over your food. As soon as you had finished, you asked gravely, 'Can we wave to her, Granny?' 'Of course, my love,' I said, and picking you up in my arms I carried you into the garden. We stood on the lawn for some time, while you waved your little hand at the stars.

1 December

Over these last few days I've been feeling thoroughly out of sorts. No particular event sparked it off; the body is like that, it has its own internal checks and balances and can be thrown out of kilter by a mere trifle. Yesterday morning when Signora Razman delivered my shopping and saw that I was depressed, she said that in her opinion it was due to the moon: there had been a full moon the night before. And if the moon can influence the tides and make the radishes in the garden grow faster, why should it not also have an effect upon our temper? What are we if not water, gas and minerals? Anyway, before she went she left me a hefty pile of trashy magazines, so I've spent a whole day stupefying myself among their pages. I fall for it every time! When I first see them I think all right, I'll glance through them for half an hour and then go and do something worthwhile. But every time, once I get stuck into them, I can't escape until I've read the last word. The unhappy life of the Princess of Monaco makes me sad, the proletarian loves of her sister make me indignant, every sob-story related with superabundant detail makes my heart beat faster. And those letters! I never cease to be amazed by what people have the nerve to write about. I'm not narrow-minded, or don't think I am, but I can't deny that the uninhibited frankness of people leaves me somewhat perplexed.

The weather is colder today. I didn't go for my walk in the garden, afraid that the sharp wind, coupled with the chill inside me, would have made me snap like a dry branch in the frost. I wonder if you are still reading this screed of mine or if, now that you know me better, you feel such repulsion that you have been unable to continue. The sense of urgency that has possessed me will allow no suppression of the facts; I cannot stop now or turn aside. Even though I kept that secret for years, I can do so no longer. When you were perplexed about not having an identity, I told you how, to begin with, I felt a similar or even greater perplexity. I know that your feeling about identity – or rather the lack of it – was closely bound up with the fact that you never knew who your father was. It was quite natural to tell you where your mother had so tragically gone, but when you questioned me about your father I was never able to give you an answer. How could I? I had not the slightest idea who he was. One summer Ilaria went to Turkey on her own for a long holiday; when she returned she was pregnant. She was already over thirty and at that age childless women can fall prey to a strange obsession. They want a child at any price; how and with whom is of no importance.

Besides, at that time most women were feminists, and your mother and some friends of hers had formed a group. Many of their ideas seemed right, they were ideas I shared, but among them there were unnatural growths, unhealthy, distorted notions. One of these was that a woman is the sole arbiter of what happens to her body. She alone decides whether or not to have a child, the man is no more than a biological necessity and should be treated as such. Your mother was not alone in what she did; two or three of her friends had children in similar circumstances. One can understand it up to a point: the power to give birth confers a sense of omnipotence. Death, darkness and insecurity recede when you usher another part of yourself into the world, and this miracle makes everything else irrelevant.

To support their contention, your mother and her friends pointed to the animals. 'The female,' they said, 'only gets together with the male at the moment of copulation, then they go their separate ways and the young stay with the mother.' I cannot confirm whether this is true or not, but I do know that we are human beings, and that every one of us is born with a face that is unique and that we carry with us throughout our life. An antelope is born with the muzzle of an antelope, a lion with that of a lion, each one identical to every other member of the species. In nature features do not change, while man, and only man, has a face. A face, you understand? The face says everything. It has your history within it, your father, your mother, your grandparents and great-grandparents, maybe even a long-lost uncle nobody can remember. Behind the face lies the personality, the good things and the not so good things you inherit from your ancestors. Our face is our initial identity, allowing us to find our place in life, saying: Here I am, this is me. So when you were thirteen or fourteen and began to spend hours at a time looking at yourself in the mirror, I knew what you were looking for. Of course you were looking at pimples and blackheads and a nose which had suddenly grown out of proportion, but there was something else besides. Discounting or thinking away the features of your mother's side of the family, you were trying to imagine the face of the man who had given you being. This was precisely the factor your mother and her friends had given too little thought: that one day the child, looking in a mirror, would realize there was someone else inside, and would want to know everything about this other person. Some people spend their whole lives trying to trace the features of their mother or father.

Ilaria was convinced that heredity played a negligible part in the development of a child, whereas education, surroundings and upbringing were all-important. I don't share this view, holding that both have equal importance. Upbringing accounts for half, what we bring with us from birth accounts for the other half.

Before you went to school there were no problems. You never asked about your father and I took care never to raise the subject. But as soon as you began to attend elementary school, what with the chatter of the other girls and the pernicious essay subjects suggested by your teachers, you became aware that there was something missing in your everyday life. In your class there were, naturally, children from broken homes and abnormal backgrounds, but none had the complete blank you had where the father was concerned. How, when you were only six or seven, could I explain to you what your mother had done? And besides, when you come down to it, I myself knew nothing except that you had been conceived in Turkey. So in order to invent a story not totally incredible, I started from the one sure fact: your country of origin.

I bought a book of oriental fables, and read you one of these each night. Using them as a model, I invented one specially for you. Do you still remember it? Your mother was a princess and your father a prince of the Crescent Moon. Like all princes and princesses they loved each other so much they were prepared to die for each other. But there were many people at the court who were jealous of such a love. The most jealous of all was the Grand Vizier, a powerful and evil man, and he it was who cast a terrible spell upon the princess and the child she was carrying in her womb. Luckily the prince had been warned by a faithful servant, so your mother was able to escape from the castle one night, dressed as a peasant woman, and found refuge here, in the city where you were born.

'I am the daughter of a prince?' you would ask me, your eyes shining. 'Indeed,' I replied, 'but it is a dark, dark secret and you must never tell anyone.' What was I trying to do with that bizarre lie? Nothing, except give you a few more carefree years. I knew that one day you would stop believing my silly fairy story. I also knew that when that happened you would in all probability begin to hate me. But it was absolutely impossible for me not to tell you the story. Even had I summoned up every last vestige of my courage, I could never have brought myself to say, 'I have no idea who your father is, and perhaps your mother had no idea either.'

Those were years of sexual liberation, when erotic activity was considered a function to be indulged in whenever one wanted to – one day with one partner, the next with another. Your mother had dozens of boyfriends, but I don't remember one who lasted more than a month. Ilaria, unstable by nature, was affected more than most by this precarious love-life. Although I never stopped her doing what she wanted, and never criticized her in any way whatever, I found this permissiveness rather worrying. It wasn't so much the promiscuity that shocked me, but the impoverishment of the senses. With the disappearance of prohibitions and the sense of individual uniqueness, passion disappeared. Ilaria and her friends reminded me of guests at a banquet suffering from bad colds and eating what is put before them out of politeness, even though all the food – carrots, roast meats, desserts – to them tastes exactly the same.

Your mother's choice was certainly dictated partly by the new permissiveness, but perhaps by something else besides. How much do we know about the workings of the mind? Quite a lot, but not everything. Who can tell if, in her deep subconscious, she had some intuitive feeling that the man she saw every day was not her father? Could much of her anxiety and instability have stemmed from this? This was a question I never asked myself when she was little, or during her adolescence and young womanhood. The fiction with which I had surrounded her was complete. But when she returned from that holiday three months' pregnant, it occurred to me that there is no escape from lies and falsehood. Or rather, you can escape for a time, but they bob up again when you least expect it, no longer as manageable as when you first uttered them believing them harmless, but transformed into horrible monsters, devouring ogres. As soon as you set eyes on them, they throw you to the ground and consume you and all around you with a terrible greed. When you were ten, you came home from school one day in tears. 'Liar!' you said to me and immediately shut yourself in your room. You had discovered that my fable was a lie.

Liar could be the title of my autobiography. I have only told one lie since the day I was born.

That lie destroyed three lives.

4 December

The blackbird is still sitting on the table in front of me. She's not eating quite as well as in the past few days. Instead of chirping at me incessantly, she sits in her box and doesn't even pop her head out any more, so all I can see are her top feathers. Although it was chilly this morning, I went to the nursery with the Razmans. I didn't make up my mind to go until the last moment: the cold would have made a polar bear think twice, and in some dark corner of my heart there was a voice asking whether it was worth planting any more flowers. But when I started to dial the Razmans' number, I noticed the faded colours in the garden and rebuked myself for being selfish. Maybe I shall not see another spring, but you will.

I've been feeling so unsettled lately! When I'm not writing I wander through the house restlessly without finding anywhere I can be at peace. Of the few things I can still do, not one gives me the remotest sense of satisfaction or succeeds for a moment in chasing away the sad memories. I have the impression that memory works a bit like a deep-freeze. You know what happens when you take out food that has been there for some time. To begin with it's as hard as a brick, odourless, tasteless, covered with a film of ice. But as soon as you heat it up it gradually regains its proper shape and colour and fills the kitchen with its smell. In the same way, unhappy memories lie dormant in the innumerable crannies of one's mind for years, decades, a whole lifetime. Then one day they surface and the pain that was part of them revives, as intense and poignant as on that day in the distant past.

It was telling you about myself, about my secret. But a story should begin at the beginning, and this one begins in my childhood, in the unusual isolation in which I grew up and which continued into adult life. When I was young, intelligence was a decidedly negative factor for a woman when it came to marriage. Custom demanded that a wife should be no more than a brood mare, passive and adoring. A woman who asked questions, an enquiring, restless wife was the last thing any man wanted, and that explains why my sense of solitude was so tremendous when I was young. To tell the truth, between the ages of eighteen and twenty, since I was not bad-looking and came from a reasonably well-to-do family, I had swarms of suitors around me. But as soon as they realized that I could hold my own in a conversation, as soon as I opened my heart and spoke about what was occupying my mind, they vanished. Of course I could have kept quiet and pretended to be something I was not, but unfortunately – or fortunately – despite my upbringing there was a part of me that was still alive, and that part refused to live a lie.

After high school, as you know, my education came to a halt because my father refused to allow me to continue. This was an enormous disappointment to me and undoubtedly why I was so avid for knowledge. As soon as a young man said he was studying medicine, I bombarded him with questions, wanting to know everything. I did the same with students of engineering and with budding barristers. This confused them greatly, because they had the impression that I was more interested in their studies than in them, and they were probably right. When I was talking to the other girls at school, I felt like a creature from another planet light-years away. The main difference between us was in the question of female guile. While I had none, they had developed theirs to the limit. Behind their arrogant, self-confident façade, men are extremely vulnerable and naïve; deep down they conceal some very primitive responses; use the right bait and they fall for it hook line and sinker. I realized this very late, but my school-mates knew it by the age of fifteen or sixteen.

They exchanged *billets-doux* as to the manner born, accepting or rejecting them, adopting a different tone at will; they arranged rendezvous and failed to turn up, or turned up late. At dances, they stroked themselves provocatively while gazing into their partners' eyes with the dreamy expression of young does. These are feminine wiles, the allurements that lead to success with men. But I, you see, was a muggins and understood nothing of what was going on around me. You may think this strange, but I had a fierce streak of loyalty in me, and this sense of loyalty told me that I should never, and I mean never, play fast and loose with a man. I believed that one day I would find a young man with whom I could talk far into the night without tiring; talking on and on, we would come to realize that we saw things in the same way, that we felt the same emotions. So love would be born, a love based on friendship, on respect, not on easy subterfuge.

I wanted a loving friendship, and in this I showed a masculine quality, virile in the old sense of the word. It was, I believe, my assumption of equality in the relationship that terrified my suitors. So, little by little, I was reduced to accepting the role that normally belongs to the plain Janes. I had a host of women friends, but the friendships were one-sided; they sought me out only as a confidante for their love problems. One after the other my friends married; there was a time when I seemed to be doing nothing but go to weddings. My contemporaries had babies, and I was always the spinster aunt; I was still living at home with my parents and I was by now almost resigned to the thought that I would be a spinster for ever. 'What's the matter with you?' my mother would say. 'What's wrong with What's-his-name or Thingummy-bob? Such nice boys!' My parents obviously ascribed my problems with the opposite sex to the eccentricity of my character. Did it upset me? I don't know.

Actually, I felt no overwhelming desire for a family. The idea of producing a child made me uneasy. I had suffered too much as a child and was afraid of causing similar distress to an innocent creature. Besides, although I was still living at home I was completely independent, every hour of the day was my own to spend as I wished. I earned a little money by coaching a few students in Greek and Latin, my favourite subjects, but apart from this there were no calls on my time. I could spend the whole afternoon in the public library without having to account for my actions to anybody, or could take myself off on holiday whenever I felt like it.

Compared to those of other women, mine was a life of freedom, and I was afraid of losing this freedom. And yet with the passage of time this freedom, this apparent happiness, came to seem increasingly false and forced. Solitude, which to begin with had seemed a privilege, began to be a burden. My parents were growing old, my father had had a stroke that left him lame. Every day I tucked his arm through mine and took him to buy a newspaper. I was twenty-seven or twenty-eight. Looking at our two reflections side by side in the shop window, I felt that I too was old, and realized the direction my life was taking. It would not be long before he died, my mother would soon follow him and I should be alone in a big house full of books; perhaps I would take up embroidery or painting in watercolours to pass the time and the years would fly past one after the other. Eventually, one morning, worried by not having seen me for a few days, someone would call the fire brigade, the firemen would force the door and find my body on the floor. I would be dead, and what remained of me would be little different from the dry carcass left on the floor when an insect dies.

I felt my woman's body fading without having lived, and this made me sad. And then I felt alone, dreadfully alone. I had never in my life had anyone to talk to, really talk to, I mean. Yes, I was certainly intelligent, I read a great deal; in the end my father used to say, with a measure of pride: 'Olga will never marry; she's got too much brain.'

But all this presumed intelligence was getting me nowhere; I was incapable of setting out on a real journey, of studying anything in depth. I felt that my intellectual growth had been stunted by lack of a university education. But the real cause of my ineptitude, of my inability to use the gifts I had, lay elsewhere. After all, Schliemann was self-taught when he discovered Troy. What really held me back was something else, the incident of that little dead dog, remember? It was he who curbed me, who stopped me from moving forward. I was standing still, waiting. For what? I hadn't the least idea.

Snow had fallen the day Augusto first came to the house. I remember it well because snow was a rare sight in our part of the world and the reason our guest was late for dinner. Like my father, Augusto was a coffee importer; he had come to Trieste to discuss the sale of our business. After his stroke my father, in the absence of male heirs, had decided to sell up and live out his last years in peace. My first impressions of Augusto were anything but favourable. He came from Italy, as the people in our region were wont to say, and like all Italians had an affected manner which I found irritating. It's a strange fact how often people who are destined to play an important role in our lives strike us initially as singularly unpleasant. After dinner my father went to lie down, leaving me to entertain our guest in the sitting-room until he left to catch his train. I was most put out. Throughout the hour or so that we were together I went out of my way to be rude to him. I replied to his questions with monosyllables, didn't speak unless he did, and when he held out his hand as he was leaving, I gave him mine with the haughty indifference of a duchess conferring a favour on a social inferior.

'He's a pleasant enough young man for an Italian, this Augusto,' commented my mother at supper that evening. 'He's a man of integrity,' my father replied, 'and also a capable businessman.' And guess what happened then? I blurted out without thinking and in a sudden access of vivacity: 'And he wasn't wearing a wedding ring!' Even before my father replied, 'Ah yes, poor man, he's a widower,' I was as red as a tomato and deeply embarrassed by my outburst.

Two days laters, when I got back after a lesson, I found a package wrapped in silver paper beside the front door. I had never received a parcel in my life before, and I couldn't imagine who could have sent it. A note had been slipped under the wrapping. It said: 'Have you tasted these before?' And was signed by Augusto.

That night, with those sweets on the table by my bed, I could not get to sleep. I told myself that he had sent them as a polite gesture to my father, and munched one chocolate after the other. Three weeks later he was back in Trieste 'on business', as he said during dinner. But this time, instead of returning immediately as he had done before, he stayed in town for a while. Before taking his leave he asked my father's permission to take me for a drive and my father gave it without even consulting me. We spent a whole afternoon driving around the city streets. He spoke little; he asked me to tell him about the various monuments and listened to what I had to say in silence. He listened; for me that was nothing short of a miracle.

On the day he left he sent me a bouquet of red roses. My mother was all excited; I pretended not to be, yet I waited several hours before opening and reading the card. Within no time his visits became weekly events. He came to Trieste every Saturday and returned to his home town on Sunday. Do you remember how the Little Prince tamed the vixen? He sat outside her den every day waiting for her to come out, so that she gradually learned to recognize him and not be afraid, and even got excited when she saw anything that reminded her of her little friend. Seduced by the same kind of tactics, I was already excited by the time Thursday arrived – the taming process had begun. In less than a month my life revolved around waiting for the weekend. In a very short time a feeling of familiarity had developed between us. Here at last was someone I could talk to, who appreciated my intelligence and sympathized with my desire for knowledge. For my part, I valued his calmness, his qualities as a listener, the sense of security and protection an older man can give to a young woman.

We were married in a simple ceremony on the first of June 1940. Ten days later Italy was at war. My mother sought the safety of a village in the Veneto mountains while I, with my husband, went to L'Aquila.

To you who have learnt the history of those years only from books, studying it rather than living it, it must seem strange that I should omit any mention of all the tragic events taking place. We had fascism, the race laws, war had broken out and yet I thought only about my own little troubles and the microscopic movements of my spirit. Don't think that my attitude was anything unusual. Far from it. Apart from a tiny politicized minority, everyone in our town was doing the same. My father, for example, who considered fascism as so much hot air and called the Duce 'the water-melon vendor' at home, went to dine in the evening with the fascist elders and stayed talking to them late into the night. In just the same way, I found the whole business of taking part in the 'Italian Saturday', having to march about and sing garbed in mourning black, ridiculous and time-wasting. But even so I went, my attitude being that it was a boring duty one had to discharge for the sake of a quiet life. There is certainly nothing heroic in such behaviour, but it is common enough. A peaceful life is one of man's greatest ambitions. It was so then and is probably so today.

In L'Aquila we lived in Augusto's family home, a large apartment on the first floor of a baronial palace in the heart of the city. The furniture was dark and heavy, there was little light and the outlook was grim. My heart sank as soon as I crossed the threshold. Is this where I am to live, I wondered, with a man I've known for only six months, in a city where I don't have a single friend? My husband understood my despondency immediately and during the first two weeks did all he could to distract me. Every other day he would get the car out and we would go for drives through the hills round the town. We both adored excursions. The sight of the beautiful mountains, of picturesque villages clustering around hilltops, had a calming effect upon me; to a certain extent they made me feel as if I had never left the North, my own home. We still talked a great deal. Augusto loved nature, particularly insects, and on our trips he explained many things. I owe nearly all my knowledge of natural history to him.

When the two weeks that constituted our honeymoon were over, he returned to work and I began my normal life, alone in the great apartment except for one servant, an old woman who saw to most of the housework and cooking. Like all middle-class wives, once I had planned the menus for luncheon and dinner, I had nothing to do. I acquired the habit of going out every day for long walks. I would walk up and down the streets at a furious pace, my head awhirl with thoughts I was quite unable to clarify. Do I love him, I asked myself, suddenly pulling up short, or has it all been a colossal mistake? When we were sitting at the dining table or in the sitting-room of an evening I would look at him and ask myself what I felt. I felt tenderness, certainly, and was quite sure he felt that for me too. But was this love? Was this all it was? Never having felt anything else, I could not answer my question.

After a month had passed, the first whispers reached my husband's ears. 'The German,' these anonymous voices said, 'walks around the streets alone at all hours of the day.' I was totally nonplussed. Having been brought up in a different environment, I had never imagined that my innocent walks could give rise to scandal. Augusto was unhappy, he understood why I found the situation incomprehensible, but for the peace of the neighbourhood and his good name he begged me to desist from my solitary walks. After six months of that life I felt drained of every vestige of vitality. The little dead dog inside me had become an enormous dead dog, I moved like an automaton, my eyes were glazed. When I spoke, I could hear my words as distinctly as if they were being spoken by someone else.

Meanwhile I had got to know the wives of Augusto's colleagues, and we met every Thursday in a coffee bar in the town centre. Although we were all about the same age, we had little to talk about. We spoke the same language, but had nothing else in common.

Re-absorbed into his own surroundings, Augusto soon began to behave like the other men of his region. We now hardly spoke during meals, and when I made an effort at conversation he replied monosyllabically with a yes or no. After dinner he often went to his club, but even when he stayed at home he would shut himself in his study to reorganize his collection of beetles. His great ambition was to discover an insect no one had discovered before, so that his name would be perpetuated for ever in scientific manuals. I would have liked to ensure the perpetuation of his name in another way, through a son. I was now thirty and felt that the sands of time were running ever more swiftly. Things were going badly in that department. After a rather disappointing wedding night, not much else had happened. I felt that all Augusto wanted was to find someone there at meal times, a woman he could show off with pride in the cathedral on Sundays; he was apparently not unduly concerned with the person behind this comfortable façade. Where had he gone, the pleasant, companionable man of our courting days? Was it possible that love could end like this? Augusto told me once that birds sing more loudly in the spring to attract a mate and get help in building the nest. He had done the same, but once I was installed in the nest he had ceased to take any interest in me. I was there, I kept the nest warm, and that was all there was to it.

Did I hate him? No. It may seem strange, but I couldn't make myself hate him. To induce hate, the person involved must wound you, harm you in some way. Augusto did nothing to me; that was the problem. You can die of nothingness more easily than you can die of pain; pain you can rebel against, but you can't rebel against nothingness.

When I spoke to my parents on the phone, I naturally told them that everything was fine, forcing myself to speak in the tone of voice that suggested a happy young bride. They were convinced that I was in good hands and I didn't want to disturb their confidence. My mother was still hiding out in the mountains, my father had remained in the family home, looked after by a distant cousin. 'Any news?' he would ask me once a month, and every time I would answer no, not yet. He was longing for a grandchild. With senility had come a tenderness he had never had before. I felt closer to him now that this change had come about, and I was sad to disappoint him. At the same time, I did not have the confidence to explain to him the reason for this prolonged childlessness. My mother wrote lengthy epistles dripping with rhetoric. 'My adored daughter,' she wrote at the top of the page, which she then proceeded to fill with a detailed account of the pathetically few things she had done on that particular day. At the end, she invariably announced that she had finished knitting the umpteenth layette for the imminent arrival. I, meanwhile, was withering. Every morning I found the reflection in the mirror uglier than the day before. In the evening I would sometimes ask Augusto, 'Why don't we talk to each other?' 'What about?' he would say, without raising his eyes from the lens through which he was examining an insect. 'I don't know,' I said, 'perhaps we could tell each other something.' He would shake his head and say, 'Olga, what funny ideas you have.'

It's a commonplace to say that dogs begin to look like their owners if they live with them long enough. I had the impression that the same thing was happening to my husband, that as time passed he was becoming more like a beetle in every way. His movements were no longer those of a human being at all; instead of being smooth they were geometrical, with every gesture accomplished in a series of jerks. And his voice was toneless, issuing with a metallic sound from some unidentifiable part of his throat. The insects and his work absorbed his attention completely, to the point of obsession; nothing else elicited the smallest degree of enthusiasm. One day he showed me a revolting insect, holding it up with a pair of tweezers. I think it was called a mole cricket. 'Look at those jaws!' he said. 'He can eat anything with those.' That night I dreamt of him in the same shape; he was enormous and was devouring my wedding dress as if it had been a piece of cardboard.

After a year we took to sleeping in separate rooms. He often stayed up late with his beetles and didn't want to disturb me, or so he said. Described like this, my marriage must seem terrible and extraordinary to you, but there was nothing extraordinary about it. At that time, almost all marriages were like this, little domestic hells in which one partner succumbed sooner or later.

Why did I put up with it? Why didn't I pack my bags and return to Trieste? Because at that time neither separation nor divorce existed. A marriage could be ended only in the case of very serious ill-treatment, otherwise one needed a real spirit of rebellion, to escape and spend the rest of one's life wandering about the world. But rebellion, as you know, is not part of my nature, and Augusto never once raised his voice to me, let alone a finger. He saw that I never lacked for anything. On our way home after Mass on Sundays, we stopped at the Nurzia patisserie and he would tell me to help myself to anything I wanted. You can imagine my feelings every morning when I woke up. After three years of marriage my one and only thought was of death.

Augusto never spoke to me about his former wife; on the rare occasions when I attempted a tentative question, he changed the subject. As time went by and as I wandered through those ghostly rooms on winter afternoons, I became convinced that Ada – for that was her name – had died not of some illness or accident but by her own hand. When the servant was out I spent my time lifting floorboards, removing drawers, feverishly seeking a clue that would confirm my suspicion. One rainy day, I found some women's clothes at the bottom of a wardrobe. They were hers. I pulled out a dark dress and tried it on. It was my size. Looking at myself in the mirror, I began to cry. I cried silently, not sobbing but like one who knows that her fate is sealed. In a corner of one of the rooms was a *prie-dieu* carved in heavy wood which had belonged to Augusto's mother, an immensely devout woman. When I didn't know what to do I shut myself in the room and knelt on it for hours with my hands clasped. Praying? I don't know. I was talking, or trying to talk to Someone I imagined was there above my head. I said, Lord let me find my path, and if this is the path I must tread, help me to bear it. Habitual attendance in church, which my married status made unavoidable, had raised a host of questions in my mind, questions which had lain dormant since early childhood. The incense made me dizzy, and so did the sound of the organ, and as I listened to the Holy Scriptures something vibrated almost imperceptibly inside me. However, when I encountered the priest away from the church and without his vestments, when I saw his swollen, spongy nose and his little piggy eyes, when I heard his banal and uncompromisingly false questions, the vibration ceased completely and I thought: there you are, it's nothing but deception, a way of helping the weak-minded to bear the oppression of their daily lives. Despite this, however, I loved to read the Gospels in the silent house. I found much of the teachings of Jesus quite extraordinary; they inspired me to the point where I would repeat them aloud over and over again.

My family was not religious in the slightest. My father prided himself on being a free-thinker and my mother, whose family had converted from Judaism two generations before, as I told you previously, went to Mass simply because it was expected of her. On the rare occasions when I asked her questions regarding religious belief, she always answered, 'I don't know. Our family has no religion.' No religion. That phrase weighed like a millstone on my most vulnerable childhood years, when I was beginning to ask important questions. The words were like a brand of infamy. We had abandoned one religion to embrace another for which we had not the slightest respect. We were traitors, and for us as for all traitors, there was no place in heaven or on earth.

So, apart from a few Bible stories told by the nuns at school, I'd had no religious instruction at all before the age of thirty. The kingdom of God is within you, I would repeat to myself as I wandered through the empty rooms. And while repeating it I tried to imagine where it was. I saw my eye reaching like a periscope into my body, probing the coils of my abdomen and the most mysterious convolutions of my brain. Where was the kingdom of God? I couldn't find it. There was a fog around my heart, a thick fog, not the luminous green hills of my imagined Paradise. In my most lucid moments I told myself I was going mad, like all old maids and widows; slowly, imperceptibly I was slipping into a mystic delirium. After four years of such a life, it was becoming ever more difficult to distinguish what was real from what was false. The bells of the cathedral nearby struck every quarter of an hour; to avoid hearing them, or at least to muffle the sound, I took to stuffing my ears with cottonwool.

I had become obsessed with the idea that Augusto's insects were not really dead. I heard the rustling of their feet everywhere around the house at night, climbing up the wallpaper, scratching their way over the tiles in the kitchen, creeping through the rugs in the sitting-room. I lay in bed holding my breath and waiting for them to crawl through the keyhole into my bedroom. I tried not to let Augusto see the state I was in. Every morning I would announce my plans for dinner with a smile on my lips, and the smile remained until he was out of the door. The same fixed smile was in place when he returned.

The war, like my marriage, was now in its fifth year. In February Trieste was bombed, and one of the very last bombs destroyed my childhood home. The only casualty was my father's carriage-horse; it was found in the garden with two of its hooves missing.

In those pre-television days news travelled more slowly than now. I learnt about the loss of the house the day after, because my father telephoned me. As soon as I heard his voice I knew something dreadful had happened; it was the voice of someone for whom life has long ceased to have any meaning. Now, with no place of my own to return to, I felt that all was indeed lost. For two or three days I wandered around the house in a daze. Nothing could shake me out of it. I saw my life unfolding before me in a long series of monotonous grey years that would continue until I died.

Do you know the one mistake we always make? It is to believe that life is immutable, that once we have set it rolling along a particular line, we have to remain on that line to journey's end. Fate has more imagination than we do: just when you feel that there's no way out of a particular situation, when you have reached the depths of desperation, with the speed of a gust of wind everything changes, is overturned, and from one moment to the next you find yourself living a new life.

Two months after the bombing of the house, the war was over. I had gone to Trieste immediately. My parents had already found temporary lodgings in a flat they were sharing with other people, and there were so many practical details demanding my attention that before a week was out I had almost forgotten about the years in L'Aquila. Augusto arrived a month later. He had to take over the running of the business bought from my father which was now severely run down, having been left in the hands of a manager throughout the war. And there were my parents, homeless and now very old. With a speed that took me by surprise, Augusto decided to quit his home town and move to Trieste; he bought this little house on a high plateau and we were all living here together before the autumn.

Contrary to all expectations, my mother was the first to go. She died in the early summer. The long years of loneliness and fear had undermined her stubborn constitution. Her death reawakened my craving for a child, and I began sleeping with Augusto again, but even so, nothing, or hardly anything, happened between us at night. I spent hours sitting in the garden with my father. It was he who said, in the course of one sunny afternoon, 'Taking the waters can perform miracles for the liver and for women.'

Two weeks later, Augusto drove me to the station and put me on the train for Venice. From there I took another train to Bologna in the late morning, and after changing once more I arrived that evening in Porretta Terme. To tell the truth, I had little or no faith in the efficacy of the waters; my decision to leave was due above all to a longing to be alone, to enjoy my own company in a way totally different from the past years. I had suffered. Inside, almost every part of me felt dead; I was like a field that has been burnt, everything was black, turned to cinders. Only exposure to rain, sunshine and wind would allow the little that was left to find – gradually – the energy for new growth.

10 December

Since you went away I've stopped reading the papers. You're not here to buy them for me, and no one else does. I missed them to begin with, but gradually it became quite a relief not to have them. I remembered Isaac Bashevis Singer's father, who said that of all the habits modern man has acquired, reading a daily newspaper was the worst. In the morning, just when his spirit is at its most receptive, it pours over him all the evil produced by the world the day before. In those days all you had to do was ignore the papers to avoid this; nowadays that's no longer possible: there's television and radio, and you only have to switch them on for a second for the evil to reach you, to crawl under your skin.

That is what happened this morning. While I was getting dressed I heard on the regional news that the convoys carrying refugees are to be allowed to cross the frontier. They had been stranded there for four days, not allowed to proceed and unable to go back where they came from. They were carrying the old, the sick, unaccompanied women with small children. According to the newsreader, the first contingent has now reached the camp set up by the Red Cross and the refugees are being provided with the essentials. I find the proximity of a war, so close to home and so primitive, deeply disturbing. Ever since it broke out I have felt as if I had a thorn in my heart. The image is banal, but with all its banality it conveys the feeling precisely. After a year, I felt not only pain but indignation; it seemed impossible that nobody would intervene to stop the slaughter. Then I resigned myself to the situation: after all, there are no oil wells in the region, only stony mountains. As time passed, indignation gave way to rage, and this rage still scratched away inside me like a stubborn mole.

It is ridiculous that I, at my age, should still be so affected by war. When all's said and done, hundreds and hundreds of people are fighting each other every single day, so in eighty years I should have been able to develop a callus of sorts, become inured. Refugees and armies (victorious or routed) have been fleeing through the tall yellow grass of the Carso since the day I was born. First there were the troop trains carrying infantrymen during the Great War, and bombs exploding on the high plateaux; then the long lines of men returning from the Russian and Greek campaigns, from Nazi and Fascist blood-baths, massacres in the trenches. And now once more the sound of heavy gunfire along the border, an exodus of the innocents fleeing from the Balkan killing-fields.

Some years ago when I was travelling in a train from Trieste to Venice, I found myself in the same carriage as a medium. She was a married woman a few years younger than me, wearing a kind of tam-o'-shanter. Of course I didn't know to begin with that she was a medium, but I gathered as much from her conversation with the woman sitting next to her.

'You know,' she said as we travelled across the Carso plateau, 'when I walk across this plateau I hear the voices of the dead; I can't take two steps without being deafened by them. They all scream horribly, and the younger they died, the louder they scream.' She went on to explain to her companion that wherever an act of violence takes place, the atmosphere is changed for ever. The air, she said, becomes corroded and lumpy, and the corrosion, instead of releasing gentle feelings in compensation, encourages further violence. 'The world,' the medium said finally, 'is like a vampire. Once it tastes blood it must have new blood, fresh blood, more and more of it.'

For years I have asked myself if this land we live in could be hiding some secret curse. I asked that question in the past and I continue to ask it now – without finding the answer. Do you remember how often we used to climb up to Monrupino? When the north-east wind was blowing we used to spend hours gazing together at the landscape; it was almost like looking down from an aeroplane. We had a 360-degree view, and competed to see who would be the first to identify a particular peak in the Dolomites or find Grado da Venezia. Now that I'm no longer strong enough to go there, I have to close my eyes to see the same view.

Thanks to the magic of memory everything appears before me and around me as if I were standing at the top of the mountain. I can even hear the wind and smell the scents of the season I have chosen. I stand there looking at the limestone columns eroded by time, the great tract of bare earth where the tanks practise their manoeuvres, the dark promontory of Istria plunging into the blue sea, and as I look at everything around me I ask myself for the umpteenth time what, if anything, strikes a discordant note.

I love this landscape, and perhaps that's why I can't answer the question; the only thing I can be certain about is that the visible surroundings influence the character of all who live in the region. If I am sometimes harsh or brusque, and if you are too, it is the Carso that is to blame, with its erosion, its colours, the wind that lashes it. Had we been born in the Umbrian hills, for instance, we might have been less abrasive and indignation would not have been in our nature. Would it have been any better? I don't know; we can't imagine a state of affairs we have never experienced.

However, there must have been some small malediction in the air today, for when I came into the kitchen I found the blackbird lying dead in her bed of rags. She had been looking peaky for some days, eating less and often dozing off between morsels. Death must have occurred just before first light, because when I picked her up her head swung limply from side to side as if a spring had broken in the mechanism. The little body was so light, so fragile, so cold! I stroked her for a minute before wrapping her in a cloth; I wanted to give her a little warmth. Outside the air was full of fine snow. I shut Buck in a room and went out. I'm not strong enough now to dig holes with a spade, so I scruffed out a trench with my shoe in the flowerbed where the earth is softest, laid the blackbird in it and then, before going back indoors, recited the prayer that you and I always used when we buried little birds: 'Lord, receive this tiny life as you have received all the others.'

Do you remember how many we cared for and tried to save when you were a little girl? After every windy day we would find at least one injured bird – chaffinches, tom-tits, sparrows, blackbirds, once we even found a crossbill. We did our best to make them better but our efforts were nearly always in vain and we would find them dead without warning from one day to the next. And how tragic it always seemed; no matter how often it happened, you were invariably upset. The burial over, you would dry your nose and your eyes with the palm of your hand, then go and shut yourself in your bedroom 'to get over it'.

One day you asked me how we were going to find your mother, because heaven was so big that people could easily get lost. I told you that heaven was like a big hotel; everyone had their own room and all the people who had loved each other on earth would, after their death, find each other in that room and stay together for ever. For a while this explanation satisfied you, but after the death of your fourth or fifth goldfish you returned to the question and asked me, 'What happens if there isn't enough space?' I replied, 'If there isn't enough space, you have to close your eyes and repeat the words "room get bigger" for a whole minute. And the room will expand immediately.'

Do you still remember these childish fantasies, or has your shell banished them? I had forgotten this one until today when I was burying the blackbird. 'Room get bigger,' what a lovely piece of magic! Indeed, what with your mother, the hamsters, the sparrows and the goldfish, your room must be as crowded already as the stands at a football match. Soon I shall be going up there too; will you want me in your room or do I have to rent a separate one nearby? Shall I be able to invite the first person I ever loved, shall I be able to introduce you to your real grandfather at last?

What were the thoughts, the images in my mind when I got out of the train at Porretta that September evening? Absolutely none. The smell of chestnuts was in the air and my only concern was to find the *pensione* where I had booked a room. I was still very naïve and had no idea about the remorseless workings of fate. If I was convinced of anything at all, it was that whatever happened to me was the result of the good or less good exercise of my willpower. The moment I stepped from the train on to the platform, my willpower dissolved, I wanted nothing, or rather one thing only – to be left in peace.

I met your grandfather on the very first evening. He was dining at my *pensione* with another man. Apart from one old gentleman, there were no other guests in the dining-room. He was arguing rather heatedly about politics, and the tone of his voice immediately grated on my nerves. I gave him a couple of decidedly hard looks during the meal. You can imagine how surprised I was the following morning to discover that he was the spa's medical officer! He questioned me for ten minutes about the state of my health, then something terribly embarrassing happened, for just as I was taking my clothes off I began to sweat as if I were doing something extremely strenuous. Listening to my heart, he exclaimed, 'Good grief, what a fright you've had!' And burst out laughing in a rather off-putting manner. When he took my blood pressure, the mercury shot up to the top, and he asked if I suffered from hypertension. I was furious with myself, and told myself over and over again that there was nothing to be afraid of, that he was only a doctor doing his job, and that getting into such a state was was neither normal nor becoming. But however much I tried, I was unable to calm down. As I left and he handed me a sheet of paper with my regime, he shook my hand. 'Rest and relax,' he said, 'otherwise not even the waters will do you any good.'

That evening, after supper, he came and sat down at my table. By the next day we were walking around the town together and chatting. The liveliness and impetuousity which had irritated me so much now began to fascinate me. There was so much passion and enthusiasm in everything he said that it was impossible to be near him without being infected by the warmth in every phrase he uttered and the warmth of his physical presence.

A long time ago I read in some newspaper that, according to the latest theories, love springs not from the heart but from the nose. When two people meet and are attracted to each other, they begin to send out little hormones – I don't remember what they're called – which enter the nostrils and rise to the brain where, in some secret convolution, they stir up storms of passion. The article concluded, in short, that feelings are nothing but invisible smells. What nonsense! Anyone who has ever felt true love, the love that can be neither measured nor described, knows that such a statement is only another of those innumerable cack-handed attempts to denigrate the heart. I'm far from denying that the scent of a person you love can arouse intense emotion, but for the emotion to be aroused something must have happened already, something that I am certain is quite different from a mere smell.

When I was with Ernesto during those days, I had the sensation, for the first time in my life, that my body had no bounds. I felt a kind of impalpable aura around me, as if my boundaries had grown larger, and that this largeness vibrated in the air every time I moved. You know what happens to plants that haven't been watered for a few days. The leaves become flaccid, and instead of lifting themselves up towards the light they droop like the ears of a depressed rabbit. Well, my life over the preceding years had been like that of an unwatered plant: the dew at night had been just sufficient to sustain life but I had had nothing else, I had the strength to stand upright but no more. But you only need to water a plant once to revive it, for the leaves to lift themselves again. This happened to me during the first week. Six days after my arrival I looked in the mirror and saw another person. My skin was smoother, my eyes brighter, and as I dressed I began to sing, something I had not done since I was a child.

Viewing this account from the outside, you are probably thinking that underneath all this euphoria there must have been some self-doubt, some anxiety, some torment. After all, I was a married woman, so how could I accept the companionship of another man light-heartedly? On the contrary, I felt no self-doubt, no misgivings, not because I was particularly liberal-minded but because what was happening to me concerned my body and only my body. I was like a puppy who has been wandering about the streets in the cold of winter for days on end and then finds a snug den; asking no questions, he curls up and enjoys the warmth. Besides, the opinion I had of my female charm was pretty low, and it never crossed my mind that a man might find me interesting in that way.

As I was walking to church on the first Sunday, Ernesto pulled up beside me in a car. 'Where are you going?' he asked, leaning out of the window, and as soon as I told him he opened the door, saying, 'Believe me, God will be much happier if, instead of going to church, you come for a good walk through the woods.' At the end of a long, winding road we came to the start of a path that disappeared among the chestnut trees. The shoes I was wearing were not designed for walking along a rough path, and I stumbled repeatedly. When Ernesto took my hand, it seemed the most natural thing in the world. We walked for a long time in silence. The scent of autumn was in the air, the earth was damp, many of the leaves on the trees had turned yellow, and the light filtering through them was toned into softer hues. After a while we came to a clearing, and in the middle of it stood an enormous chestnut tree. Remembering the oak tree of my childhood I went up to it, first stroking it with my hand, then laying my cheek against it. A second later Ernesto laid his cheek next to mine. Our eyes had not been so close since we had known each other.

On the following day I didn't want to see him. Friendship was developing into something else and I needed time to think. I was no longer a young girl but a married woman with the responsibilities of a married woman; he too was married and, what's more, he had a son. I had already predicted my life until my old age; the fact that something unforeseen was now disturbing these predictions caused me great anxiety. I didn't know what to do. The unexpected always alarms at first; to go ahead you have to get over the fear. So one moment I would be thinking: This is quite absurd, I must forget what has happened, blot out the little there has been so far; and the next I would be telling myself that it would be even more absurd to break off now, when I had come alive for the first time since I was a child, when everything was vibrating around me and inside me. To give it all up seemed a total impossibility. I naturally had misgivings, the suspicion that occurs – or used to occur – to every woman, that he was leading me on, that he wanted to amuse himself and no more. All these thoughts were whirling in my head as I sat alone in that dingy rented room.

The following night I couldn't get to sleep until about four o'clock. I was too agitated. In the morning, however, I wasn't in the least tired, and began to sing as I got dressed. A tremendous love of life had invaded my whole being in those few hours. On the tenth day of my stay I sent Augusto a postcard: *The air is wonderful, the food mediocre. Hope all well.* And sent him an affectionate kiss. I had spent the previous night with Ernesto.

During that night I had became aware of the existence of

a number of tiny windows between the soul and the body through which, when they are open, feelings can flow. If they are just ajar, emotions can only trickle through; only love can fling them wide open all at once like a violent gust of wind.

We were never apart during the last week of my stay in Porretta; we went for long walks and talked until our throats were dry. What a difference between Ernesto's way of speaking and Augusto's! Everything about Ernesto was passion, enthusiasm. He could talk about the most complex subjects with total simplicity. We often spoke about God and the possibility of something beyond tangible reality. He had fought in the Resistance and had looked death in the face more than once; moments such as these had made him think about the idea of a superior being, not out of fear but from a sense of enlarged consciousness. 'I avoid church ritual,' he told me, 'I never go into any place of worship and I shall never believe in any religious dogmas or in stories invented by men no different from myself.' We took the words out of each other's mouths, thought the same thoughts, expressed them in the same way. It was as if we had known each other for years instead of only two weeks.

We had very little time left. Those last nights together we hardly slept, dozing just enough to regain our strength. Ernesto became passionate about the subject of predestination. 'In the life of every man,' he said, 'there is only one woman with whom he can achieve the perfect union, and in the life of every woman there is only one man with whom she can become complete.' Few, however, were destined to meet each other; the rest were forced to live in a state of dissatisfaction, of perpetual yearning. 'How many such encounters are there?' he asked in the darkness of the room, 'one in every thousand? one in a million? one in ten thousand?' Yes, one in every ten thousand. All the others are matters of compromise, of superficial and ephemeral attraction, of physical affinity or compatibility of character, of social convention. Having reached this conclusion, he said nothing apart from repeating, over and over again, 'Aren't we lucky? I wonder what's behind it all. Who knows?'

On the day I left, waiting together for the train in the tiny station, he embraced me and whispered in my ear, 'In what previous life did we meet?' 'In many,' I said, and began to weep. Hidden in my handbag I had an address where I could write to him in Ferrara. I shan't even attempt to describe my feelings during the long hours of the journey; they were in too much of a turmoil, too 'one alone against the whole world'. I knew that I had to effect a metamorphosis in those hours, so I went backwards and forwards to the toilets to check the expression on my face. The light in my eyes and my smile had to fade. The flush on my cheeks had to be the only remaining proof that the air had done me good. My father and Augusto both found the improvement extraordinary. 'I told you the waters would do you good,' my father kept repeating, while Augusto, for the first time in his life, surrounded me with little attentions.

When you first experience love, you will understand how various and how odd the effects can be. When you are not in love with anybody, when your heart is free and your eyes seeking nobody else's, of all the men you might find attractive not one takes any interest in you. The moment you are claimed by one person and no one else matters a fig, the men start to run after you, whispering sweet nothings and paying court. It's those little windows I was telling you about that have this effect; when they are open the body sheds a great light upon the soul and the soul upon the body, they illuminate each other by a system of mirrors. Very soon you have a warm golden halo around you which attracts men like bears to honey. Augusto was no exception and, strange though you may think it, I had no difficulty in responding with kindness. Of course, had Augusto been more a man of the world, a bit more shrewd, he would have realized what had happened. For the first time since I married him I found myself being grateful to his revolting insects.

Did I think about Ernesto? Of course – I did little else. But thinking is not the right word. Rather than thinking, I existed for him, he existed in me, in every movement, in every thought we were one person. When we parted we had agreed that I should be the first to write; before he could write to me I had to find a trustworthy woman friend to whose address he could send his letters. The first letter I sent to him was at the end of October. The period that followed was the worst in our whole relationship. Not even the greatest, most absolute love can be wholly exempt from doubts when the lovers are far apart. Every morning I would wake, suddenly and completely while it was still dark outside, and lie motionless and silent beside

Augusto. These were the only moments when it was unnecessary to hide my feelings. I thought about those three weeks. And what if Ernesto, I wondered, were only a seducer, a man who, out of boredom at the spa, made a habit of amusing himself with unaccompanied women? The longer I waited for the letter that didn't come, the more my suspicion transformed itself into a certainty. Very well, I told myself, even if it has turned out like this, even if I behaved like the most naïve of silly women, the experience was neither negative nor without use. Had I not let myself go, I should have grown old and died without knowing what a woman can feel. There was a sense, you see, in which I was trying to protect myself, to soften the blow.

My father and Augusto both noticed my increasingly bad temper. I would fly off the handle for no reason and leave the room as soon as one of them entered it. I needed to be alone. I went over and over the weeks we had spent together, subjecting them to a frenetic minute-by-minute scrutiny in my efforts to find a clue, something that would enable me to make up my mind once and for all. How long did this torture last? Six weeks, nearly two months. Finally, the week before Christmas, the letter arrived at the house of the friend who was acting as go-between. Five pages covered with a bold, flowing hand.

My good humour was restored immediately. Writing and waiting for replies made the winter fly past and the spring too. The constant thought of Ernesto altered my perception of time; all my energies were concentrated on a vaguely defined future, on the moment when I would see him again.

The depth of feeling in his letter had put my mind at rest about the love we shared. Ours was a great, an enormous love, and like all truly great loves it was largely unaffected by mundane events. It may seem strange to you that the long separation should not have made us dreadfully unhappy. It would be untrue to say that we did not suffer at all; both Ernesto and I suffered from the enforced separation, but other feelings were mixed in with the pain, and the expectation of meeting again pushed the pain of separation into the background. We were both grown-up, married people, and we knew that things could not be otherwise. Had it happened in these last few years, I would probably have asked Augusto for a separation before a month was out, he would have separated from his wife and we would have been living in the same house before Christmas. Would that have been better? I don't know. Deep down I can't get over the idea that if relationships are too easy, love becomes trivialized and the intensity of passion is degraded to a passing fancy. You know what happens to a cake if the yeast isn't mixed in properly; instead of rising uniformly, it bulges on one side or cracks, allowing the mixture to run out of the mould like a stream of lava. That is what the uniqueness of love is like – it overflows.

To have a lover and manage to see him was not a simple thing in those days. For Ernesto it was, of course, easier; as a doctor he could always plead a meeting, a conference, an urgent case, but for me, who had no activity apart from that of housewife, it was almost impossible. I had to invent an excuse, some reason to absent myself for a few hours or even days without arousing suspicion. So just before Easter I joined a club for amateur Latinists. The members met once a week and made frequent excursions to places of cultural interest. Knowing my love of ancient languages, Augusto suspected nothing and had no reason to be critical; he was happy to see me renewing an old interest.

The summer arrived in a flash that year. At the end of June Ernesto left home for the spa season, as he did every year, and I went to the coast with my father and husband. During that month I managed to convince Augusto that I still wanted a child. Early on the thirty-first of August, he drove me – carrying the same suitcase and wearing the same clothes as the year before – to the station to catch the train for Porretta. Throughout the journey I was too excited to sit still for a moment. From the window I saw the same landscape I had seen the year before, yet everything was different.

I stayed at the spa for three weeks, and in those three weeks I lived more profoundly than in the whole of the rest of my life. One day, walking alone in the park while Ernesto was working, I thought how wonderful it would be to die at that moment. It may seem strange, but the greatest happiness, like the greatest unhappiness, often gives rise to this contradictory desire. I felt as though I had been walking along cart-tracks through the woods for years and years; I'd had to hack my way through the undergrowth with a machete, and could see little except what was immediately in front of me; I didn't know where

I was going, or what lay ahead of me, which could have been an abyss, a great city or the desert; then all at once I had emerged to find that, without realizing it I had been climbing upwards and was now standing on the top of a high hill. The sun had just risen and other hills of different hues dropped towards the horizon. Everything was tinged with misty blue, a light breeze played upon the summit, the summit and my head, my head and the thoughts inside it. Every now and then a sound rose from the valleys below, the barking of a dog, the chiming of a bell. Everything was strangely light and intense at the same time. Inside me and around me everything had become clear, nothing was hanging over me, there was nothing to cast a shadow. I had no desire to go down again, to descend into the undergrowth; I wanted to immerse myself in the blue mist and stay there for ever, end my life at this, the supreme moment of my existence. I was still thinking along these lines in the evening when I met Ernesto. I didn't dare raise the subject during dinner, however, for fear that he would laugh at me. But late that evening, when he joined me in my room, when he put his arms around me, I put my lips close to his ear intending to say, 'I want to die.' Instead, what I said was 'I want a baby.'

When I left Porretta I knew I was pregnant. I think Ernesto knew too, for in the last few days he had seemed troubled and confused and had frequently fallen silent. My body had begun to change the very morning after I conceived. My breasts had suddenly become fuller and firmer, my complexion more luminous. It is amazing how quickly one adapts physically to cope with the new situation. This is why I can say that even without a pregnancy test and even though my stomach was as flat as ever, I knew perfectly well what had happened. I felt as though I were flooded with radiance, my body was adjusting itself, beginning to expand, to become imbued with power. I had never felt anything like it in my life before.

More solemn thoughts came to my mind only when I was alone on the train. While I was with Ernesto I had never doubted that I would have the baby. Augusto, my life in Trieste, local gossip, all that was very far away. Now, however, that world was coming closer, and given the rapidity with which my pregnancy would develop, I had to make decisions at once and, once taken, stick to them. I realized that to have an abortion would – paradoxically – be much more difficult than to have the baby. Augusto could hardly fail to notice if I had an abortion, and what explanation could I give having insisted for so long that I wanted a child? Besides, I had no wish for an abortion. The tiny being growing inside me had not been a mistake to be corrected at the earliest opportunity, but the fulfilment of a desire, possibly the most deeply felt desire of my life.

When you love a man, when you love him with the whole of your body and your soul, there is nothing more natural than wanting a baby. This is a not a desire prompted by the intelligence, not a rational choice. Before meeting Ernesto I fancied that I would like a child and knew exactly why I wanted it and all the pros and cons. That was a rational choice. I had wanted a child because I was getting on and was very much alone, because I was a woman and women, if they do nothing else, can at least have babies. Had I been buying a car I would have applied precisely the same criteria.

But that night when I told Ernesto that I wanted a baby, it was something quite different. This was a decision flying in the face of common sense, yet it was stronger than all the arguments common sense could muster. Besides, when you come down to it, there was no decision involved, only a frantic, avid desire to possess in perpetuity. I wanted Ernesto inside me, with me, near me for ever. Now, reading about how I behaved, you will probably be shuddering with horror and asking yourself how you could have failed to notice that I was hiding such a base, despicable side of my nature. When I arrived at the station of Trieste I did the only thing I could do, which was to act like a tender wife in love with her husband. Augusto was struck by the change in me, and instead of looking for explanations became a willing participant.

After a month it was entirely plausible that the child was his. The day I announced the result of the test he came home at mid-morning and spent the whole day with me planning what changes to make to the house before the baby's arrival. When I shouted the news in my father's ear, he took my hands in his dry ones and stood there for a while, his eyes becoming damp and red. For some years now his deafness had been a barrier between himself and much of what went on around him, and his conversation was in fits and starts with sudden long gaps between one phrase and the next, full of scraps and fragments of the past that no longer had any relevance. I don't know why, but instead of moving me his tears roused a subtle sense of repugnance. I saw them as a gesture, nothing more. But he never saw his granddaughter. He died in his sleep, without pain, when I was in the sixth month of pregnancy. When I saw him laid out in the coffin I was struck by how shrivelled and worn he was. His face had the same expression as always, distant and neutral.

I wrote to Ernesto, naturally, as soon as I knew the result of the test; the reply came back in less than ten days. I waited several hours before opening the letter. I was very agitated, afraid it might contain something disagreeable. It was late afternoon before I plucked up courage enough to find out, and I shut myself in the cloakroom of a bar to do so in peace. His words were calm and reasonable. 'I'm not sure if this is the best thing to do,' he wrote, 'but it is your decision and I respect it.'

Now that all the problems had been resolved, I began a peaceful preparation for motherhood. Did I feel that I was a monster? Was I one? I don't know. During the pregnancy and for many years afterwards I suffered neither doubts nor remorse. How did I manage to feign love for one man while carrying in my womb the child of another whom I truly loved? Things are never that simple, they are never all black or all white, but made up of many different shades. It was never difficult for me to be gentle and affectionate towards Augusto because I was genuinely fond of him. I loved him in a way quite different from the way I loved Ernesto, not with the love of a woman for a man, but rather the love of a sister for an older and rather boring brother. Had he been vicious in any way everything would have been different, I should never have dreamt of having a baby and living in the same house, but he was only very methodical and predictable; and besides, he was essentially good and gentle. He was happy about the child, and I was happy to bear it for him. What motive was there for revealing my secret? That would have destroyed the happiness of three people. At least, that is what I thought at the time. In these days of freedom and choice, what I did may well seem dreadful, but at the time the circumstances were quite usual. I don't say it happened to every married couple, but it was not a particularly rare thing for a woman to conceive a child outside wedlock. And what happened? The same as happened to me: absolutely nothing. The child was born, grew up in the same way as the other children in the family and achieved adult status untroubled by the slightest suspicion. At that time the family was a solid entity, and it took much more to destroy it than the presence of a child different from the rest. And this happened in your mother's case. As soon as she was born, she was my daughter and Augusto's. The most important consideration for me was that Ilaria was the result of love and not chance, social convention or boredom. This, I thought, would pre-empt any other problem. How wrong I was!

For the first few years, however, life proceeded normally without any great upheavals. I lived for her and was – or thought I was – a fond and attentive mother. From the first summer of her life I got into the habit of spending the hottest months of the year with the child on the Adriatic coast. We rented a house and every two or three weeks Augusto would spend the weekend with us.

Ernesto saw his daughter for the first time on that beach. He had to pretend to be a complete stranger, of course. Walking along the beach he 'happened' to walk close to us; he chose a chair shaded by an umbrella a few steps away, and from there (when Augusto was not with us) he observed us for hours on end while pretending to be absorbed in a book or newspaper. In the evening he wrote me long letters describing everything that had gone on in his head, his feelings for us, all that he had seen. In the meantime, his wife had also had a child, their second; he had resigned from the seasonal work at the spa and set up a private practice in Ferrara, his home town. During Ilaria's first three years we did not meet apart from those seemingly chance encounters. I was engrossed with the child, waking every morning happy in the knowledge that she was there; even had I wanted to, I could not have concentrated on anything else.

Shortly before we parted at the end of my second stay at the spa, Ernesto and I had made a pact. 'Every evening,' he said, 'at eleven o'clock precisely, wherever I am and whatever the circumstances, I shall go outside and look for Sirius. If you do the same, than even if we are far, far apart, even if we have not seen each other for a long time and know nothing about what the other is doing, our thoughts will meet up there and will be close.' We went out on to the balcony at the *pensione* and from there, tracing a path with his finger through the stars, he showed me Sirius glittering between Orion and Betelgeuse.

12 December

Last night I was woken by a sudden noise, but it took me a while to realize that it was the telephone. By the time I got out of bed it had been ringing for some time and stopped just as I reached it. I picked it up nevertheless and said 'Hello' two or three times in a sleepy voice, then instead of going back to bed I sat in the chair by the phone. Was it you? Who else could it have been? That sound in the middle of the night had shaken me. I recalled a story told me by a friend a few years ago. Her husband had been in hospital for a long time, and the day he died, because the visiting rules were strict, she hadn't been with him. That night she was too upset to sleep, and as she lay there in the dark she suddenly heard the phone ring. She was naturally surprised, thinking it most unlikely that anyone would be ringing up at that hour to offer condolences. As she reached out her hand towards the phone, she was struck by something very odd: the phone had a kind of halo of shimmering light around it. The surprise, however, turned to terror when she raised the receiver. She heard a voice that seemed to come from very far away and to speak with great difficulty. 'Marta,' it said against a background of hissing and crackling, 'I wanted to say goodbye before I went . . .' It was her husband's voice. Immediately afterwards she heard a noise like a loud wind; it lasted only a second, then the line went dead and all was silence.

At the time I excused my friend's flight of fancy knowing how deeply distressed she was, though the idea of the dead communicating with the living by means of modern technology struck me as distinctly bizarre. But the story must have left its mark upon me nonetheless. Deep down inside, really very deep down inside, in the most ingenuous and susceptible-to-magic part of my being, perhaps there lurks a wish that sooner or later someone might telephone me from the Great Beyond. I have buried my daughter, my husband and the man I loved most in the world. They are dead, they no longer exist, and yet I continue to feel like a survivor from a shipwreck. The tide has washed me up safely on an island and I know nothing about my companions who disappeared when the ship capsized; they may have drowned – indeed it is more that likely – but perhaps they haven't. Although months and even years have passed, I continue to gaze at the nearby islands expecting to see a puff of smoke, a signal, something to confirm my suspicion that they are still alive and part of the same world.

The night Ernesto died I was woken up by a very loud noise. Augusto switched the light on, calling out 'Who's there?' But there was nobody in the room, and everything was in its rightful place. It wasn't until I opened the wardrobe door the next morning that I found all the shelves had collapsed and my stockings, shoes, scarves and knickers were in a heap at the bottom.

Now I can talk about 'the night Ernesto died', but at the time I didn't know. I had only just received a letter from him and nothing could have been further from my mind. I merely supposed that the battens holding up the shelves had rotted with damp and given way under the weight. Ilaria was four years old, she had just started kindergarten and my life with Augusto and her had settled into an ordinary humdrum existence. That afternoon, after a meeting of the Latinists' Club, I went to a bar to write to Ernesto. There was to be a conference in Mantua in two months' time, and this was the chance to meet we had both been looking forward to for a long time. I posted the letter on my way home and the following week I was expecting his reply. No letter came that week or during the ensuing weeks. He had never kept me waiting so long before. To begin with I assumed the letter must have been lost in the post, then that he must be ill and unable to go to his surgery to collect his mail. A month later I wrote him a short note, but there was still no reply. As the days passed I began to feel like a house undermined by water seeping into the foundations. To begin with the seepage was a trickle, seemingly innocuous, barely lapping at the concrete supports, then it became bigger, more forceful, more turbulent until the concrete turned to sand and the house, even though it still stood and appeared to be sound from the outside, was ready, I knew, to crumble at the slightest push, which would have sent façade and all crashing to the ground like a house of cards.

By the time I left to go to the conference I was a shadow

of my former self. Having put in the briefest of appearances in Mantua, I went straight to Ferrara where I tried to find out what had happened. No one answered the door at the surgery, and from the street the shutters looked firmly closed. On the second day I went to a public library and asked to see the newspapers of the last few months. There, summed up in a terse paragraph, was all I needed to know. Returning one night from a visit to a patient, he had lost control of the car and hit a large plane tree. He died almost immediately. The date and time corresponded exactly with the collapse of my wardrobe.

In the horoscope section of one of those dreadful magazines that Signora Razman brings me every now and then I once read that Mars in the eighth house presides over all violent deaths. According to the article, no one born under this planetary configuration is destined to die peacefully in his or her bed. One wonders if Ilaria and Ernesto were born under this sinister combination. Twenty years apart, father and daughter died in exactly the same way, crashing into a tree at the wheel of a car.

Ernesto's death threw me into a profound depression. I immediately realized that for the past few years I had been shining not by light emanating from within myself but by reflected light. The happiness and love of life I had felt did not belong to me at all, I had merely functioned as a mirror. Ernesto had radiated light and I had reflected it. With him gone, all was dark once more. The sight of Ilaria no longer brought me joy but only irritation. I was so disturbed that I even doubted she was really Ernesto's child. My change of attitude did not escape her. With the sharp antennae of a sensitive child she registered my rejection and became wilful, demanding. She was now the young, vital creeper, I the old tree whose life was about to be sapped from it. She sniffed out my guilty feelings like a bloodhound and turned them into hooks for her tendrils. The house became a little hell of quarrels and shouting matches.

To relieve me of the burden, Augusto hired a woman to look after the child. He had tried for a time to get her interested in his insects, but after three or four attempts – seeing that her only response was to cry 'They're revolting!' – he had given up. Augusto was showing his age; he might have been his daughter's grandfather rather than her father; he was kind but distant. Every time I saw myself in the mirror I noticed that I, too, had aged greatly. My features had taken on a harshness they had never had before. Neglecting myself was a way of showing my self-disgust. Now with school and the woman taking Ilaria off my hands, I had plenty of time to myself, and as my unhappiness made me constantly restless I would take the car and drive myself up and down the Carso in a kind of trance.

I re-read some of the books on religion that I had begun to study in L'Aquila, seeking frenziedly for an answer to my problems in their pages. I strode about repeating to myself the words of St Augustine on the death of his mother: 'Let us not grieve for her loss, but rather give thanks for having known her.'

A woman friend had put me in touch with her confessor, but on each of the two or three occasions we met I came away feeling more dispirited than before. His words were sickly sweet; he eulogized the power of faith as if it were a foodstuff available from the corner shop. I could not find a reason for Ernesto's death, and the darkness within me made the search even more difficult. You see, when we met, when we fell in love, I had immediately felt that everything was resolved, I was happy to be alive, I rejoiced in the existence of everything around me, I felt that I had arrived at the peak of my existence, that it was solid and that nothing and nobody could shift me from it. I had the cocky assurance of people who think they know it all. For years I believed that I had reached this point by my own endeavours, but in fact I had not taken a single step unaided. Even though I had not realized it at the time, I had been carried on the back of a horse; it was he who had advanced along the road, not I. The moment the horse disappeared I became conscious of my own feet and of their frailty; I wanted to walk but my ankles gave way, my steps were the stumbling steps of a small child or an old person. For a while I thought of laying hold of any prop that was to hand: religion, for instance, or work. I soon discarded the idea, knowing that I would be blundering yet again. At forty years of age there's no longer room for blunders. If you find yourself naked, you have to be brave enough to accept the fact: I had to begin all over again. Fine, but where from? From myself. Easy enough to say, but how difficult to put into practice! Where was I? Who was I? What was the last time I was truly myself?

As I've already said, I walked for hours on the hills overlooking the city. Sometimes, when I felt that solitude was only making me more unhappy, I returned to the town and walked up and down the main thoroughfares, mingling with the crowds and seeking some kind of relief. It was almost like having a job, for I left the house when Augusto left and returned when he returned. My doctor told me that this need for movement was a normal part of certain types of nervous breakdown. I was not suicidal, so there was no risk attached to my perambulations; the exercise, he said, would eventually have the effect of calming me. Augusto accepted his explanation, but whether he believed it or was deliberately turning a blind eye in the interests of a quiet life, I do not know; still, I was grateful to him for standing aside and not obstructing my agonized wanderings.

The doctor was quite correct in one thing. However depressed I was, I was not suicidal. It was strange, but not for one moment after Ernesto's death did the thought of killing myself enter my head. It was not Ilaria who held me back, for as I told you before, she meant nothing to me at the time. It was rather a gut feeling that my sudden loss was not, was not meant to be, an end in itself. Somehow it had to have a purpose, and I glimpsed this purpose presenting itself to me like a high ledge which I had to reach. Was it there to be surmounted? Probably, though I could not imagine what was on the other side or what I should see once I reached the top.

Out in the car one day, I came to a place where I had never been before. There was a tiny church surrounded by a small cemetery, the hills on either side were covered with woods, and on the top of one of these I could see the grey walls of an old fort. Just beyond the church were two or three rural dwellings; hens scratched freely about in the road, a black dog was barking. The name on the map was Samatorza. Samatorza . . . the name sounded like Solitude – the right place to collect one's thoughts. A rough stony path led out of the village, and I began to walk along it without a thought for where it might lead. The sun was already setting, but the farther I walked the less I wanted to stop. Every now and then the screech of a jay made me jump. Something ahead was calling me, but what it was I understood only when I reached a clearing and saw standing in the middle, tranquil and majestic, its arms outstretched as if to welcome me, an enormous oak tree.

It sounds silly, but as soon as I saw it my heart began to beat in a different way; rather than beating, it seemed to be purring like a happy little cat; it used to beat in that way only when I saw Ernesto. I sat down underneath it, stroked it and leant my back and head against the trunk.

Know thyself. I wrote those words as a schoolgirl on the first page of my Greek exercise book. Sitting beneath the oak tree the long-buried phrase resurfaced in my mind. Know thyself. Fresh air, breath of life.

16 December

It snowed in the night; the garden was white when I woke up this morning. Buck rampaged over the lawn like a mad thing, leaping about, barking, seizing branches with his teeth and tossing them in the air. Signora Razman came round later; we had a cup of coffee and she invited me to spend the evening of Christmas Day with them. 'What do you do all day?' she asked me before she left. I shrugged my shoulders. 'Nothing,' I replied. 'I watch a little television, I think a little.'

She never asked after you; she skirts around the subject tactfully, but I can hear from the tone of her voice that she thinks you've been ungrateful. In the middle of a conversation she often remarks that young people are heartless, that they no longer show respect. To cut her short I nod, but privately I am convinced that hearts are what they always were; there's less hypocrisy, that's all. Young people are no more naturally selfish than old people are naturally wise. Understanding and superficiality have nothing to do with age but with the life that each of us leads. I don't remember where, but not long ago I read of an American-Indian saying that goes, 'Before you judge a person, walk in his moccasins for three moons.' I thought it was so good that I wrote it down on the pad by the telephone so I wouldn't forget it. Seen from the outside, many people's lives seem flawed, irrational, even mad. If we look no deeper than the surface, it is easy to misunderstand people and their relationships. Only by looking below the surface, by walking in their moccasins for three months, can we hope to understand their motives, their feelings, what makes them act one way rather than another. Understanding comes from humility, not the pride of knowledge.

I wonder if you will put on my slippers after reading this account? I hope so, I hope that you will spend a long time walking round the house in them, that you will go many times around the garden, from the walnut tree to the cherry tree, from the cherry tree to the rose, from the rose to those ugly black firs at the bottom of the lawn. I hope you will do this, not because I want to beg for your charity or to ask for a posthumous pardon, but because it is necessary for you and your future. To understand whence we came and what lies in our past is the first step towards tackling the future without falsehood.

I should have written this letter to your mother, but I am writing it to you instead. Had I not written it at all, my existence would indeed have been a failure. To make mistakes is natural, but to go to one's grave without having understood them is to make life a pointless exercise. The things that happen to us are never ends in themselves, gratuitous. Every encounter, every event no matter how small, has a meaning, and self-knowledge comes from a readiness to accept these encounters and events, and from the ability to change direction from one moment to the next, to slough an old skin as lizards do when the season changes.

Had I not remembered, on that day in my fortieth year, the phrase written in my Greek exercise book, had I not drawn a line under the past before carrying on with my life, I should have gone on repeating the same mistakes over and over again. To banish the memory of Ernesto I might have taken another lover, then another and another; in search of another Ernesto, in the attempt to find again what I had once had, I might have tried dozens. None would have matched the original and I should have continued, eternally unsatisfied, until I became a ridiculous old woman surrounded by young men. Or I could have come to hate Augusto, who was, when all's said and done, the reason why I had been unable to take more drastic decisions. Can you understand? There is nothing easier than to find a way out when you cannot face the truth about yourself. You can always shift guilt on to someone else's shoulders, but it takes courage to accept that the guilt – or rather the responsibility – is ours and ours alone. And yet this, as I have said, is the only way forward. If life is a journey, the journey is uphill all the way.

At forty years old I knew where I had to start, but to understand where I was going was a long process, full of pitfalls but fascinating. You know, watching television and reading the papers, I'm always seeing or hearing about the current proliferation of gurus, and the news is full of people who make snap decisions to follow their teachings. I get frightened by the spread of such cults and the methods they propound for finding inner peace and universal harmony. They are the visible signs of a great and widespread sense of bewilderment. We are slowly – not all that slowly – coming to the end of a millennium; even though the date is no more than a convention, it makes people think. Everyone is waiting for something tremendous to happen and they want to be ready for it. So they seek out their gurus, enrol themselves for courses in self-knowledge and after less than a month their heads are swollen with the arrogance that marks the prophets – the false prophets. Yet another big, frightening lie to add to the innumerable ones that have gone before!

The only teacher, the only true and credible teacher, is conscience. To hear its voice you have to stand in silence – alone and in silence – on the bare earth, naked and with nothing around you, as if you were dead. To begin with you can hear nothing and all you feel is terror, but then you hear a quiet voice coming from far, far away, and maybe, to begin with, you will hear only irritating banalities. It's a strange fact, but when you expect to be confronted with important things, all you see are unimportant ones, so petty and self-evident that you want to cry, 'Is this all there is to it?' If life has a purpose, the voice will whisper, the purpose is death, everything revolves around it. What a wonderful discovery, you will remark at this point. What a wonderful, macabre discovery, except that every person alive knows that he or she will die. Quite true, we all know it intellectually, but to know something intellectually and to feel it in your heart are two completely different things.

When your mother was attacking me in her hard-nosed way, I used to say, 'You are making my heart ache.' She would laugh. 'Don't be ridiculous,' she would reply, 'the heart is a muscle; as long as you don't rush about, it can't ache.'

When she was old enough to understand, I tried so often to speak to her and explain the sequence of events that led to my withdrawal from her. 'It is true,' I said, 'that I neglected you for a time when you were very small. I was seriously ill. Had I tried to look after you during the illness, it might have been even worse. But now I'm well, and we can talk, discuss things, make a fresh start.' She didn't want to know. 'Now it's me who is ill,' she said, and refused to say any more. She hated my calmness and constantly tried to ruffle me and drag me into the little pits she dug for herself every day. She had decided that unhappiness was her natural state, and put up barriers around herself to prevent anyone blurring the image she had of her own life. Rationally, of course, she said she wanted to be happy, but by the time she was sixteen or seventeen she had blocked any possibility of change. While I was discovering further dimensions, she stood with her hands covering her head, waiting for something to fall on her. My newly-discovered sense of calm irritated her; when she saw the New Testament on my bedside table she snapped, 'Why on earth do *you* need consolation?'

When Augusto died she didn't even want to attend his funeral. During the last few years of his life he had suffered from a quite severe form of arteriosclerosis; he shambled around the house talking baby-talk and she found this unbearable. 'What does this gentlemen want?' she would shout as soon as he appeared, shuffling in his slippers, at the door of a room. She was sixteen when he died, and had not called him 'papa' since she was fourteen. He died in hospital one November afternoon; he had been admitted the day before because he'd had a heart attack. I stayed in the ward with him; he was dressed not in pyjamas but in a white hospital gown tied at the back. According to the doctors, he was already over the worst.

A nurse had just brought in supper when, as if he had seen something, he suddenly got out of bed and took three steps towards the window. 'Ilaria's hands,' he said, staring with unseeing eyes. 'No one else in the family has hands like hers.' Then he returned to bed and died. I looked out of the window. A thin rain was falling. I stroked his head.

For seventeen years, without dropping a single hint, he had known.

It's midday, the sun's shining and the snow is melting. Patches of yellow grass have appeared on the front lawn and drops of water are falling one by one from the branches of the trees. I noticed something very strange when Augusto died: that death, in itself, does not always cause the same kind of grief. There is a sudden emptiness – the emptiness is always the same – but within that very emptiness different kinds of grief take shape. Everything that we did not say materializes and dilates, and gets bigger and bigger. The emptiness has no doors or windows or escape routes; whatever is suspended inside it will remain there for ever, above your head, with you, around you, enveloping and confusing you like a thick fog. The fact that Augusto had known about Ilaria but had said nothing to me disturbed me deeply. Now I wanted to talk to him about Ernesto, of what he had been to me; I wanted to speak about Ilaria, to discuss a million and one things with him, but it was no longer possible.

Perhaps you can understand now what I told you at the start — that it is not the absence of the dead that weighs upon us but everything left unsaid between us and them.

I sought the comfort of religion after Augusto's death as I had after Ernesto's. I had recently become acquainted with a German Jesuit a few years older than me. Realizing, after we had met once or twice, that I was uncomfortable with services in the church, he suggested that we should meet somewhere else. Since we both loved walking, we decided to go on walks together. He came to collect me every Wednesday afternoon, wearing heavy shoes and carrying an old rucksack. He had a face that I found very pleasant: the hollow-cheeked, serious face of a man born and bred in the mountains. That he was a priest made me shy to begin with; I told him only the half of every story, afraid of scandalizing him, of exciting condemnation or hasty judgements. Then one day, when we were resting on a rock, he said: 'You are hurting yourself, you know. Only yourself.' From that moment I stopped lying and opened my heart in a way I had not done with anyone since Ernesto's death. The words came tumbling out, and as they did so I forgot that he was a man of the cloth. In contrast to the other priests I had known, he never used words of blame or consolation; all the sickliness of the usual platitudes was foreign to him. There was about him even a kind of harshness that could be off-putting at first. 'We can only grow through pain,' he said, 'but pain has to be met head on. Those who turn aside or indulge in self-pity must inevitably lose the battle.'

Win, lose, military terms that conjured up a silent struggle, an inward fight. According to him, a man's heart is like the earth, half in sunlight and half in shadow. Not even the saints were all light. 'The simple fact that we have bodies,' he said, 'means that we are partly in shadow. We are like frogs, amphibians, because one part of us lives in the depths here below while the other reaches upwards. Living only means being conscious of this, knowing it, struggling to keep the light from disappearing, overcome by the darkness. Distrust those who think they are perfect, who think they have all the answers. Distrust everything except what your heart tells you.' I listened, fascinated. I had never before met anyone who could express so well the feelings that had disturbed me for so long and that I had been unable to put into words. Listening to him, my thoughts took shape, all at once I saw the road before me and to journey along it no longer seemed impossible.

Every now and then he would put a book that was particularly dear to him into his knapsack, and when we stopped to rest he would read passages from it in his clear, hard voice. In his company I came to know the prayers of Russian monks, the oration of the heart, and to understand passages from the Gospels and the Old Testament that had previously seemed obscure. In the years since Ernesto's death I had indeed been making an interior journey, but the path was restricted to knowledge of myself. At one point on that path I had found myself facing a blank wall; I knew well that on the other side of the wall the path stretched onwards, wider and more brightly lit, but I didn't know how to climb the wall. One day a sudden shower drove us to seek shelter in the mouth of a cave. 'What does one do to acquire faith?' I asked him. 'One doesn't do anything. It comes. You already have it, but your pride prevents you from admitting it. You ask too many questions. You make complex what is simple. In reality you have a terrible fear. Relax, and what must come will come.'

After our walks I returned home more confused, more uncertain than before. He was very harsh, as I told you, and his words wounded me. Many times I wanted never to see him again, and decided on the Tuesday evening that I would ring him and tell him not to come, that I was unwell. I never did though. Wednesday afternoons found me waiting for him at the door with my knapsack and walking shoes.

Our trips lasted rather more than a year, then, without any warning, his superiors moved him away.

What I have told you may have given you the impression that Father Thomas was an arrogant man, that there was an exaggerated fervour, even fanaticism, in his words or his vision of life. But it wasn't so. Basically he was the most placid, the mildest man I have ever known. He was no militant Christian. If there was any mysticism there, it was a personal, positive mysticism anchored in everyday reality. 'We are here, now,' he was always saying.

He handed me an envelope on the doorstep. Inside was a postcard with a picture of mountain pastures. Over the picture were the words, 'The kingdom of God is within you,' and on the back, in his handwriting, 'Under the oak tree be not yourself but the oak tree; in the woods be the woods; on the grass be the grass; among people be with people.'

The kingdom of God is within you. Remember? The same phrase that had made such an impression upon me when I was an unhappy bride in L'Aquila. Then, when I closed my eyes and looked inside myself, I could see nothing. Something changed after I met Father Thomas. I still couldn't see anything but the darkness was no longer absolute, there was a faint light in the distance and every now and then for a split second I managed to forget myself. The light was faint, weak, a tiny flame that the lightest breath would have snuffed out, but the fact that it was there at all gave me a strange feeling of weightlessness and a sensation that was not happiness but joy. Not euphoria nor exaltation, I didn't feel wiser or uplifted, all I felt growing inside me was a calm consciousness of existence.

On the grass be the grass, under the oak be the oak, among people be a person.

20 December

Preceded by Buck, I went up to the attic this morning. I can't even remember how many years ago I last opened that door! There was dust everywhere and great cobwebs hanging in the corners of the beams. Shifting the boxes and cartons, I discovered two or three nests of dormice, but they were sleeping so soundly they noticed nothing. As children, we all love attics; as old people we like them less. What used to be a place of mystery, of discovery and adventure, becomes filled with sad memories.

I was looking for the Christmas crib, and had to open several boxes and the two big trunks before I found it. I also came upon Ilaria's favourite doll, carefully wrapped up in newspapers and old clothes, and some of her toys.

Underneath I found Augusto's insects – still shiny and perfectly preserved – his magnifying glass and all his collecting paraphernalia. Nearby, in an old sweet tin, I found Ernesto's letters tied up with a red ribbon. There was nothing of yours; you are young, alive, your place is not yet in the attic.

Opening packages stored in one of the trunks I also found the few things from my own childhood that had been salvaged from the ruins of our house. They were scorched and blackened, and I pulled them out gently as if they were holy relics. Most of them were bits and pieces from the kitchen – an enamel basin, a blue-and-white china sugar-bowl, a few pieces of cutlery, a baking tin and, right at the bottom, the leaves of a book, loose and with no cover. What book could that be? I couldn't remember until I picked it up, very carefully, and glanced over the first few lines. Then it all came back to me. And what a moment that was! This wasn't just any old book, but the one that I had loved best of all as a child, the one that had fed my fantasies more than any other. It was called *The Marvels of the Twenty-first Century* and was, in its way, a work of science fiction. The story was simple enough but full of imagination. Two scientists living at the end of the nineteenth century and, wanting to know whether all the wonderful things promised by progress would really come about or not, arranged to be preserved in a state of hibernation until the year two thousand. After exactly one hundred years, the grandson of a colleague (a scientist himself) thawed them out and took them on a tour of the world on board a flying platform. There were no extraterrestrials or spacemen in this story; everything that happened was concerned solely with man and his fate and what he had built with his own hands. And, according to the writer, man had done a great many things, all wonderful. Hunger and poverty had disappeared from the world since science, aided by technology, had found ways of making every corner of the globe fertile and – what was even more important – had ensured equitable distribution to all its inhabitants. Machines took the hard drudgery out of work, everyone had a great deal of free time, so every human being could cultivate his or her noblest faculties. The world resounded with music, poetry and calm, learned philosophical discussion. As if this were not enough, the flying platform could whisk you in less than an hour from one continent to another. The two old scientists were very pleased. Everything their positive philosophy had led them to hypothesize had come about. Leafing through the book I found my favourite illustration: the two rotund scientists, with their Darwinian beards and checked waistcoats, gazing delightedly down from their flying platform.

To remove the last shred of doubt, one of the two plucked up courage to ask the question nearest his heart: 'And what about the anarchists and the revolutionaries? Do they still exist?' 'Oh certainly they do,' replied their guide with a smile. 'They live all by themselves in cities under the polar icecaps, so they couldn't harm other people even if they wanted to.'

'And what about the armies?' asked the other immediately. 'I can't see a single soldier anywhere!' 'There are no more armies,' the young man replied.

The two old ones breathed a sigh of relief. At last Man had returned to his original state of goodness! But their relief was short-lived, because their guide immediately went on to say, 'Oh no, that's not the reason. Man has not lost his passion for destruction, only learnt to control it. Soldiers, guns and bayonets are things of the past. Their place has been taken by a small but extremely powerful weapon, and it is entirely due to this that wars are a thing of the past. You have only to climb a mountain and drop it from a height to make the whole world collapse into a pile of splinters and tiny fragments.'

Anarchists! Revolutionaries! What nightmares those words conjured up when I was a child. This may be difficult for you to understand, but you must remember that I was seven at the time of the October Revolution. I heard adults whispering terrible things among themselves, and one of my friends at school told me that the Cossacks would soon be in Rome, at St Peter's, and would water their horses at the sacred fountains. My sense of horror, natural to all childish minds, became obsessed with that mental picture; at night, when I was about to go to sleep, I could hear hooves thundering down the road from the Balkans.

I little knew that the horrors I would witness would be quite different and much more terrifying than horses galloping through the streets of Rome! When I read that book as a child, I did some complicated calculations to see if I would live to the year two thousand. Ninety seemed a fairly great age, but not impossible to reach. The notion gave me a certain sense of elation and made me feel superior to those who would not make it to the twenty-first century.

Now that it's nearly here, I know I shan't live to see it. Does that make me feel sad or nostalgic? No, only weary. Of all the wonders mentioned in the book I have only seen one become reality, the tiny and immensely powerful weapon. I can't tell whether it happens to other people at the end of their lives, this sudden feeling of having lived too long, seen too much, felt too much. I can't tell whether stone-age man felt the same or not. When I think about the almost full century I have lived through, my impression is that time has started to run faster. A day is still a day, the length of the night is still proportional to the length of the day, the length of the day is still governed by the seasons. It is the same as it was in the neolithic age. The sun rises and sets. Astronomically, if there is any difference at all it is minuscule.

And yet I have the impression that everything has speeded up. History is so full of happenings, it bombards us with events of every description. At the end of each day we become progressively wearier; at the end of our lives we are exhausted. Think about the October Revolution and communism! I saw the rise of communism, and the thought of the Bolsheviks kept me awake at night; I saw it spread into country after country and divide the world into two vast segments, this one black and that one white – black and white engaged in a perpetual struggle against each other – a struggle which made us all hold our breaths; the mighty weapon had been used once and might be used again at any time. Then, quite suddenly, on a day like any other, I turn on the television and learn that it is all over, they are knocking down walls, removing barbed-wire and statues. In less than a month the great utopia of the century had become a dinosaur, had been embalmed, had been rendered harmless and immobile; it stands in the middle of a hall and everyone files past it saying how big it was, oh, how terrible!

I spoke of communism, but I could just as well have

spoken about any one of a number of things, for so much has happened during my lifetime, only to disappear again. Can you now see why I said that time is moving faster? In the stone age hardly anything happened in one lifetime. The season of rain, then of snow, the season of sun and of plagues of locusts, some bloody skirmishes with the nastier neighbours, perhaps the arrival of a small meteorite in a smoking crater. Nothing existed beyond one's own pastureland, the river; with knowledge of the world so limited, of course time moved slowly.

'May you live in interesting times,' says a Chinese proverb. An expression of friendliness? I do not believe so; rather a curse. The interesting times are the troubled ones, those when many things happen. I have lived in interesting times, but you may live in even more interesting ones. An astronomical convention it may be, but the turn of the millennium always seems to bring disaster.

On the first of January in the year two thousand, the birds in the trees will wake at the same time as they did on 31 December 1999; they will sing the same songs and when they have sung them they will go, as they did the day before, to look for food. But for human beings it will be different. Maybe – if the expected disaster hasn't come about – they will set to with a will to build a better world. Will they? Perhaps, but again perhaps not. The signs I have seen so far have all been different and mutually incompatible. Sometimes I see man only as a great ape at the mercy of his instincts, unfortunately capable of using sophisticated and extremely powerful machines; at other times I have the impression that the worst is over and that the nobler side of his nature is beginning to emerge. Which hypothesis is correct? I wonder. Maybe neither is; maybe it will really come about that heaven, on the first night of the year two thousand, will punish man for his stupidity and for the less than intelligent way he has wasted the earth's resources by pouring a terrible rain of fire and brimstone upon it.

In the year two thousand you will only be twenty-four and will see all that happens. But I shall have gone by then, taking my unsatisfied curiosity with me to the grave. Will you be prepared, will you be able to deal with the new era? If a fairy floated down from the sky at this moment and offered me a wish, do you know what it would be? I would ask her to change me into a dormouse, a little bird, a spider, something small enough to live close to you but invisible. I don't know what your future holds and I can't imagine it even if I try, and because I love you it grieves me not to know. On the few occasions when we spoke about it, you certainly didn't see it as rosy. With the conviction of adolescence, you were sure that the unhappiness then persecuting you would persecute you for ever. I am convinced of the precise opposite. Why, you will ask, what signs cause me to entertain such a mad idea? Buck, my darling – nothing more and nothing less than Buck. Because when you chose him at the dogs' home you thought that you had only chosen a dog among dogs. But during those three days you were fighting a bigger, more decisive battle, between the promptings of vanity and those of the heart, and you, without doubt and without hesitation, chose to follow your heart.

At the age you were then, I would probably have opted for a silky, elegant dog, the most aristocratic-looking and sweetest-smelling one there, a dog that would turn all heads when I took it for a walk. My insecurity, coupled with the way I had been brought up, had already made me a prey to the tyranny of appearances.

21 December

After all that poking about in the attic, in the end I brought down only the crib and the cake tin salvaged from the fire. I understand the crib, you will say, because it's coming up to Christmas, but why the cake tin? This cake tin belonged to my grandmother, your great-great-grandmother, and is the only thing left of the female side of our family history. After so long in the attic it had got very rusty, so I took it straight to the kitchen, put it in the sink and tried to clean it with a liberal application of elbow grease and several soap-pads. Think how often in its life it has gone in and out of the oven, how many different cookers it has visited, each more modern than the last, how many different yet similar hands have filled it with mixture. I brought it down so that it could live again, so that you could use it and maybe bequeath it to your daughters, because in its small useful way it sums up the story of generations.

As soon as I saw it at the bottom of the trunk I remembered the last occasion when we were happy in each other's company. When was it? A year ago, possibly rather more. Just after lunch you came into my room without knocking; you found me resting on my bed with my hands clasped on my chest, and as soon as you saw me you burst into an uncontrollable fit of weeping. Your sobs woke me. 'What's the matter?' I asked as I sat up. 'What's happened?' 'It's that you're going to die soon,' you said, crying harder than ever. 'Oh dear, not that soon, I hope,' I said, laughing, and added, 'Do you know what we'll do? I shall show you how to do something that I can do and you can't, so that when I'm not here any longer you can do it and remember me.' I got up and you threw your arms round my neck. 'Now then,' I said to defuse the emotional charge that was affecting me too, 'what shall I teach you?' You dried your tears, thought about it and said, 'Let's make a cake.' So we went to the kitchen and we began a long battle. First, you didn't want to put on a pinafore, and said, 'If I wear that I shall have to wear hair curlers and carpet slippers as well. Yuk!' Then when it came to beating egg whites until they were stiff, you complained of your wrist aching; you got cross because the butter wouldn't combine with the egg yolks, and because the oven was never hot enough. I got some chocolate on the tip of my nose when I licked the wooden spoon after melting the chocolate. Seeing it, you burst out laughing. 'At your age, isn't that a bit infra dig?' you said. 'You've got a brown nose just like a dog's!'

To make one simple cake we took the whole afternoon and the kitchen looked as if it had been hit by a bomb. There was an atmosphere of bonhomie between us, a cheerfulness born of complicity. Only when the cake was finally in the oven, when you were watching it darken slowly behind the glass door, did you suddenly remember why we had made it and burst into tears again. There in the kitchen I tried to comfort you. 'Don't cry,' I said. 'Of course I shall die before you, but when I'm no longer here I'll be here all the same, I shall live in your happy memories. You will look at the trees, the vegetable patch, the flowerbeds, and remember all the good times we had together. As you will if you sit in my armchair, or if you bake the cake I taught you today and see me before you with a chocolate-brown nose.'

22 December

This morning, after breakfast, I went to the sitting-room and began to set up the crib in its usual spot next to the fireplace. First I spread out the green paper, then I arranged the dried moss, the palm trees, the stable with Joseph and Mary, the ox and the ass, and around it the groups of shepherds, the goose girls, the musicians, the pigs, the fishermen, the cocks and hens, the sheep and the goats. Over the top I fixed – with sticky tape – the dark blue paper for the sky; then, with the star of Bethlehem in the right-hand pocket of my dressing gown, and the Magi in the left, I went to the other side of the room and hung the star on the sideboard; underneath it, a little way away, I arranged the kings and the camels in single file.

Do you remember? When you were little, with the uncompromising logic peculiar to small children, you refused to let me put the star and the three kings near the crib at the beginning. They had to start from as far away as possible and advance a little at a time, the star slightly ahead and the three kings just behind it. In the same way, you couldn't bear to see Baby Jesus in the manger before it was time, so we had to make him fly down from heaven into the stable at midnight on the dot. While I was setting out the sheep on their little green mat, I recalled something else you loved to do with the crib, a game you invented and never tired of playing. It must have been Easter that first gave you the idea, because I used to hide your coloured eggs in the garden. At Christmas, instead of eggs you hid lambs, taking one from the flock when I wasn't looking and hiding it in the most unlikely place, then you would come to find me and start bleating in the most piteous little voice. So the search would start. I left whatever I was doing and, with you laughing and bleating behind me, went all over the house calling, 'Where are you, little lost lamb? Help me find you so that I can carry you to safety.'

And now, little lamb, where are you? You're over there with the coyotes and the cactus as I write; when you read this you will, in all probability, be here and my things will already be in the attic. Will my words have carried you to safety? I am not so presumptuous as to think so; perhaps they will only have irritated you and confirmed the already poor opinion you had of me before you went away. Perhaps you will only be able to understand when you are older, if you have made that mysterious journey that leads from intransigence to compassion.

Please note that I say compassion, not pity. If you ever feel pity for me, I shall come back as a wicked little sprite and vex you mercilessly. I shall do the same if you are humble instead of being modest, or if you waste your time on empty chatter when you should be silent. Light bulbs will explode, plates will fly off their shelves, knickers will drape themselves over lampshades, and from dawn until late at night I shall not leave you in peace for an instant.

No, not true. I shan't do anything. If I'm still somewhere, and if I can see you, I shall only feel sad, as I do every time I see a life thrown away, a life in which the path of love has been blocked. Take care of yourself. Every time you see a wrong you want to put right, remember that the first revolution – and the most important – has to happen inside you. To fight for an idea when you have no clear idea about yourself is one of the most dangerous things you can do.

Every time you feel lost or confused, think of the trees and how they grow. Remember that a tree with a great leafy crown and shallow roots will fall in the first gust of wind, and in a tree with abundant roots and a scanty crown the sap cannot flow freely. Roots and crown must grow in due proportion; you have to be part of things and above them; only thus can you offer shade and shelter, only thus can you put forth flowers and fruit in due season.

And when you come to a meeting of many ways and do not know which to choose, do not choose at random, but pause and reflect. Breathe with the trusting, deep breaths you took when you first came into the world; let nothing distract you, but wait and go on waiting. Be still and listen in silence to your heart. When it has spoken to you, rise up and follow it.